OUT & ALLIED

An Anthology of Performance Pieces by LGBTQ Youth and Allies

Edited by Cathy Plourde, Meghan Brodie, Sophia Glass,
Micah Malenfant, Jennifer Hodsdon, and Emmy Raviv
with Tess Van Horn and Vanessa Romanoff

addverb Publications

add**verb** Publications

A division of add**verb** Productions, a program of the Westbrook College of Health Professions, University of New England

PO Box 3853
Portland, ME 04104

www.addverbproductions.org

(207)772-1167

ISBN-13: 9780991352814 (add**verb** Publications)
ISBN-10: 0991352815
LCCN: 2011903268

Photo Credit
Johnny Speckman (pg.1, 27, 45, 73, 101, 135 and back cover)
Shannon Zura (pg.23, 41, 49 and 55)

GLSEN's LGBTQ Glossary used by permission
Translate Gender's Identity Spectrum Pinwheel used by permission

This book is dedicated to Maine's youth.
Stay brave, stay strong, stay true.

We also dedicate this book to Thom Harnett,
Maine's former Assistant Attorney General,
who has made safety for Maine youth a priority.

"Like many people my heart ached when I read of the suicide of Tyler Clementi, an 18-year-old freshman at Rutgers. It also ached when I read of what are referred to as the self-inflicted deaths of two 13-year-old boys, Seth Walsh of California and Asher Brown of Houston. The list goes on.

We need to acknowledge that while the final act might be self-inflicted, the anti-gay torment that leads to those moments plays out right in front of us in schools, online and in our communities. All members of our society, gay, straight or otherwise, need to speak up, speak out, and lend a caring hand by becoming allies for gay youth to prevent tragic stories like these from ever being told."

Thom Harnett, *Assistant Attorney General for Civil Rights Education and Enforcement*

Table Of Contents

i   *Acknowledgements*
iv   *Welcome Allies!*

2   **Proud** by Lauren Kidd
4   **Understand** by Anonymous Youth Artists Team
8   **A Phone Call** by Rai Silverstein
11   **Throwing** by That Uppity Theatre Company
17   **The Crayola Crusade** by John Coons
21   **Wishes** by Bells
24   **Our Uttermost Important Gift** by Kayla Cowan
26   **Rationalizing** by Shawna Searles
30   **The Straightest Gay Man in the World** by Micah Malenfant
34   **Dining Out** by Vianca Yohn
42   **For the Rest of My Life** by Andrew Cole
46   **Erin** by Elizabeth Peek/Wykes
47   **After Breakfast** by Meghan Brodie*
54   **To The Boy Who Yelled** by Marie Coyle
57   **If I Speak** by Rob Greatness
58   **GREY** by Mea Tavares
62   **We Fly Like Butterflies in Harmonic Symphony** by Kayla Cowan
65   **I'm Not Gay, But Thanks!** by Meredith Lamothe
70   **Personals** by That Uppity Theatre Company
72   **Pain** by Alex Eisenhart
74   **Tranny Next Door** by Carrie-Lynne Davis
82   **Absolving Yesterday** by Jake Johansen
85   **Jeopardy** by Elyse Spike Johnson
88   **Sock it to Me, Baby** by Cathy Plourde*
93   **The Girl I Kiss in Bus Seats** by Marianna Bueti
96   **Liquid Gender Form** by Stephen M. Feest
100   **Run Away** by Brianna Suslovic
102   **What Makes a Man?** by Micah Malenfant
103   **The Serpent** by Megan E. Jackson
121   **Linda** by Joan Lipkin*
125   **Once Again** by Elyse Spike Johnson
126   **Natural Stance** by Victoria Baker
128   **Tea With Dad** by Cathy Plourde*
136   **Tough Guys Wear Pink** by Stephen M. Feest

Out & Allied Handbook

PRESENTING

145   **Out & Allied in Your Community**
146   **Directing 101**
148   **Sample Audition Sheet**
149   **Rehearsals and the Rehearsal Process**
151   **How to Blow It, Served Three Ways**
153   **Taking Out & Allied on the Road**

PRODUCING THE EVENT

155   **Theatre for Civic Dialogue & Social Change**
157   **The Power of the Post-Show Discussion** by Meghan Brodie*
159   **Anatomy of a Talk-Back**

WRITING

165   **Getting Started Writing a Production-Worthy Piece**
169   **addverb Submission Release Form**

LEADERSHIP

174   **Interview with Danielle Smith** by Micah Malenfant
177   **The Right to Establish a GSA in Public Schools** by GLAD
181   **Glossary of LGBTQ Terms**
186   **Identity Spectrums** by Translate Gender

LGBTQ YOUTH THEATRE

189   **That Uppity Theatre Company**
190   **A Letter from Someone Who's Been There** by Joan Lipkin*
193   **Q&A with Brian Guehring of Rose Theatre**
194   **LGBTQ & Allied Organizations**
208   **LGBTQ & Allied Places, Spaces & Faces**
213   **Performance Pieces By The**me

216   About addverb Productions

Denotes adult contribution.

Acknowledgements

The list of who made this possible is so long and covers so many years.

*In addition to add**verb's** supporters from the last decade, there were a few grant-makers that made this book possible: the National Recreation Foundation (thank you, Katie!), the Maine Community Foundation's Equity Fund, and the Mukti Fund.*

The people who paved the way to make it safe and du jour to have GSAs— Betsy P., Maine would not be the same without your work and the support of GLSEN and the GSA Network.

add**verb** *has to thank the partner organizations who have made this possible—the team at Hardy Girls Healthy Women and their work on Ugly Ducklings; Boys to Men, Maine Youth Action Network, the agencies from Maine Coalition to End Domestic Violence and the Maine Coalition Against Sexual Assault, SALT Institute for Documentary Studies, SPACE Gallery, and CampOUT Maine, and all of the other partners we've worked with along the way. Thanks to Jim K. and Steve G. at Bernstein, Shur & Nelson. Sid & Lauren at Proactive Resources get a very special shout for the book design. We couldn't have done what you've done!*

There are many friends who have helped get us to this place as well— Meghan B, Elizabeth B., Norma B., Clara P., Katie D. & Lyndon C., Ellen L., Sage H., Gabe D., Sarah H., Jaime McL., Joan L.—and more allies and inspirations than can be listed.

add**verb's** *interns (Devon, Bre, Sophia, Andrew, Micah and the amazing Emmy), the AmeriCorps*Vista Volunteers (Hannah Legerton, Tess van Horn, Vanessa Romanoff),* add**verb's** *staff (Brandi Mathis, Amanda Bailey, Marcie Parker, Kris Hall), as well as the Board of Directors can all claim some responsibility for this book. Thank you to our new family at the University of New England's Westbrook College of Health Professions for a warm and allied welcome. Thank you to our editing weekend volunteers (Kara Larson, Donna Gasper, Paisley Richard, Julia Underwood, Bre Chamberlain Kennedy, Jen Hodsdon) who put the polish on the work.*

Thank you most of all, to the young people who took part in playwriting workshops, field testing, writing, performing and directing. Without you, this would not be.

And all of this is on the backs of those who have come before us in acts of bravery, and those who have died for being true to themselves.

Let's do it again.

"When Cathy Plourde, Director of add**verb** *Productions, approached Proactive Resources Design (PRD) to collaborate on the Out & Allied youth literary project, we could not say "yes" fast enough! We felt that more people in the gay business community should be donating their time & resources for an underserved segment of gay society: gay youth.*

It is a sad fact that in society today, gay youth have very few public role models. Finding an ally & personal advocate is a difficult exercise that may result exposing oneself to ridicule, embarrassment & even physical harm. Therefore, gay youth are a high-risk segment of gay society that should be protected & encouraged to seek out positive gay mentors & allies, and have a safe & non-judgmental place where they can be accepted as themselves and be equal to their peers.

PRD is a proud sponsor and driving force behind the DownEast Pride Alliance (DEPA), a gay business networking event in Portland, Maine, where gay, gay-friendly & young gay professionals can congregate monthly for community building & gay networking. We encourage young professionals to be a part of the gay dialogue and build on the inroads of what older gays have established thus far within their communities. While we cannot cater directly to gay youths per se, once they reach young adulthood, we do offer a supportive & nurturing safe place at DEPA where friends can mix & mingle and be a part of the local gay fabric.

Reaching out to gay youth is as easy as volunteering at gay outreach programs, mentoring gay youth at work, in your church or place of worship, or donating your time & money to gay youth programs in teen centers or with activist groups. Get involved and make a difference in someone's life, you just might save that troubled teen's life and give more meaning to your own. Your community needs you, and someone has to stand up for those whose voice is timid or non-existent. We are fortunate that today our country is a land of many colors, which when put together, form a rainbow. The question stands: How many colors do you want in your rainbow?"

Sid Tripp, *President & CEO*
Proactive Resources Inc, Co-Founder of
The DownEast Pride Alliance (DEPA)

Welcome Allies!

Welcome to those who are in, out, uncertain, or hopelessly heterosexual*!

Probably, if I were you, I'd skip this introduction and just start reading the poems and monologues and plays. I often start in the middle.

However, we're hoping the writings and sidebars will be useful, if you do get around to reading them! You could consider this section here the director's final pep talk before you head onto the stage opening night, a combination of "don't forget to…" and "breathe" and "hold for the laugh" and "support each other out there" and "please—PROJECT to the back of the house!"

First, though, before I give my version of the director's pre-show pep talk, I'd like to answer a question we get ALL the time:

> *"What does* 'add**verb**' *mean?"*

add**verb** Productions is a program, formerly a small non-profit and now a program of the University of New England. add**verb** does theatre for health and wellness education on topics people find difficult to talk about, and even more difficult to know what to do about. "add**verb**" means adding the action—adding the verb—because frankly it's not enough to just raise awareness. Most of us are painfully all too aware of what is not working, what is not fair, and what is super-challenging. The pertinent question is: what are we going to *do* about it?

> *"Bullying happens." "People are mean."*
> *"That's just how it is—deal with it."*

Okay, fine. Yes. Let's deal with it, because it's time to stop the harassment and hurt before another young person decides to take their life, or before someone decides to take it from them—all because they were or were perceived to be Lesbian, Gay, Bisexual, Transgender, Questioning or Queer (LGBTQ).

Just to be clear, "hopelessly heterosexual" is a jokey way to say that someone just knows they are born straight, and will always be straight… just the way that some people are born knowing they are not heterosexual. None of this is to say that one's understanding of their sexuality or gender is a fixed thing; for some, who they are and how they feel continues to evolve over their lifetime.

Put that way, it sounds quite dramatic, but it's actually way too real. But are we really going to settle for "that's just how it is?" Just because LGBTQ youth have been putting up with name calling and verbal taunts and rejection and physical threats and actual violence because that's been "just how it is" for a very, very long time, it doesn't mean we should throw up our arms in despair, at a loss for how one or two people, or one small unfunded Gay Straight Alliance or one church youth group can change things. That's dramatic in the bad, throw-yourself-on-the-train-tracks kind of way. We recommend choosing a different course of action, a different verb.

Got Drama?
The Out & Allied Project was designed to help you to use dramatics in the good way—to use performance as a positive action.
- An Out & Allied performance serves to *share* new and different perspectives.
- It can *challenge* the status quo.
- The pieces *model* how things could be, even if reality hasn't quite caught up.

Theatre has that power.

Each Out & Allied performance and post-show program is yours to create and define, but consider this formula to guide you:

Give people a touching moment (or several),
    followed by a big laugh,
        followed by a compelling call to action,
            add a civil discussion,
                and top it off with local resources, ideas of where one can get support, and how to pitch in to help.

Where Do You Stand?
There is an advocate who has collaborated with add**verb** over the years who works with high school and college students dealing with relationship issues. She talks about dating abuse, but what she says fits for LGBTQ support as well: If we as bystanders do not say or do anything when we see someone being harassed or hurt, we have chosen to side with the abuser; we have not chosen to stand with the victim. It made me think. What have I done when someone was being put down, whether they were in the room

to receive the verbal punches or if people were talking behind their back? And what about when physical violence moved in on top of emotional or verbal abuse—what have I done to stop or defuse a dangerous situation? Am I satisfied with what I chose to do, or do I wish I had done something differently? We mere mortals don't have the advantage of super powers—so what are we to do? WWWWD (What Would Wonder Woman Do)? or WWBMD (What Would Batman Do)?

In some cases I'm satisfied with how I handled myself, and in other cases I think I could've been a much better ally to people who don't conform to gender or sexual orientation boxes.

No one is asking you to be a super hero. Instead, please just be an ally.

Okay—an Ally. What Does It Mean Exactly?
It depends. Being an ally might mean marching in a parade or attending a Pride event. That's good, sure, but parades don't happen every day and allies are what LGBTQ youth need *every* day. Being an ally might mean showing up in small ways, or in big ways. It could mean risking being unpopular if you say something. It could mean losing friends if you refuse to hang out with people who gay-bash. It –gasp!—might even mean being called gay yourself if you stick up for someone who looks like they aren't in the heterosexual camp. Never mind that we all know you can't tell by looking!

But isn't risking popularity or being called gay a small price to pay to be able to look yourself in the eye in the morning when you are brushing your teeth?

Start Off Stage Right
There are no small parts, only small actors. What you say and what you do matter. Let's start with what you say. This might be enough to qualify as ally material:

> *"I didn't like what that person said to you in the hall—it made me uncomfortable and I can only imagine how you felt."*

Or maybe this:

> *"Hey—enough with the potty-mouth hate-speech. Don't talk that way, please."*

Or, this one's pretty good:

> *"Ah, sorry, but actually just because someone is gay it doesn't mean he likes all males…in fact, I happen to know this fellow is particular and you are definitely not his type."*

But sometimes simply saying something isn't enough. Sometimes you want to do something bigger, more active, and some of us actually don't care for parades no matter what the occasion. You need a verb, an action. Sometimes, you just have to put on a show.

Out & Allied—The Musical

Actually, there isn't any music in the book, but that doesn't mean you can't use music. The pieces in this book are (almost) all written by young people. add**verb** challenged the writers to do more than tell the story of what it means to be young and not a heterosexual. We asked them to explore what it means to support a friend or family member who could use some understanding. And, we were looking for pieces that celebrate how fabulous it is to enjoy life's best perks—love and acceptance—and find a way to not only survive, but to thrive.

It is impressive that all of the writers gave full release of their rights to these plays, poems, and monologues—a very generous action. Why did they do that? Well, to be honest, if we didn't have their permission we couldn't publish their work, so maybe some simply wanted to say "Hey, I'm a published author!" but I'd like to think that these writers were moved by the opportunity to put their labors of love and activism into your hands, to let you find the best way to use their work in your community. Because, there's a lot of work to be done to make it a safer, happier place for LGBTQ youth.

Just to acknowledge this up front: We know you will make changes, additions, and deletions to these performance pieces, and that's okay. We do ask you for one thing as you make the performance your own, though. Ask yourself, "Have I kept the spirit or intention of the writer's work?" and be able to say yes, to the best of your ability, you have. In this situation, I try to imagine the playwright will actually see it, and I want him or her to be happy with my creative interpretation of his or her work.

Yes, But Out & Allied Should Have Included One About...

True. This is just the tip of the iceberg. We've just left the trailhead. We've hardly even scratched the surface. You get the picture. There is much that is missing from this book that reflects what we need to know about being allies, and what others need to know about the lives of LGBTQ youth. So, if you note a glaring omission, you should write it—maybe get some friends to workshop it, do some improv, help it along. Then you should perform it. And then, please send add**verb** the final copy with a release form (see the back of the book for an example), and we'll put it on the website and probably also in the next book. That simple! What are you waiting for?

It might be good for all of us to remember that being young or being LGBTQ isn't a "problem" to fix or solve, but for some of us, it's just how we are, and it's pretty terrific. You probably already know that, but add**verb** is hoping that these performance pieces can help others to know it as well.

And the Ugly

It isn't all going to go perfectly. Some performers will take the production more seriously than others. Some directors will let it get to their heads. A principal might give permission but then change his or her mind to hold the pep rally instead. A jerk in the back row will make rude noises during the whole show. The bake sale concessions will be enough for 300 and only 30 will come. Or, worse.

Find a way to work through this; it is a great distraction to stay annoyed or angry for too long. Instead, get curious. Instead of being upset, or assuming the worst intentions, really try and imagine what the other person might be going through that you don't know and can't see.

From that above list of possible problem scenarios, here's an example of asking a question—being curious—and some possible reasons for what happened:

One person is taking the work more seriously than others.
>   **Curious!** Why does it mean so much to one person?
>   **Possibility?** It's really personal, maybe?

One person isn't taking the performance seriously at all.
>   **Curious!** Is there a reason why someone wouldn't be fully committed?
>   **Possibility?** Are there other pressures or fears in their way?

A director is acting like a dictator.

> **Curious!** What is the overbearing and controlling director really worried about?
>
> **Possibility?** Is it possible they are worried about how the performance will be received?

The assembly you worked forever and a day to convince the principal to give you is cancelled.

> **Curious!** What pressure might the principal have that would make him/her reverse the decision—what might you not know?
>
> **Possibility?** Any chance that more than one parent called to yell at her last night on the phone when their youth told them about a mandatory GAY assembly?

A charming fellow in the back row is rude and disruptive during the show or talk-back.

> **Curious!** What reasons would someone have to make sure that others around him or her knew that he/she didn't want to have anything to do with the performance?
>
> **Possibility?** Okay, it might be a bit obvious…you know what they say about those who "protest too much." It seems that more often than not those who have the biggest objection to non-heterosexuality are acting out of fear of the possibility they are gay themselves.

Only 30 people came to the performance. Or three.

> **Curious!** Why was the turnout so low?
>
> **Possibility?** The people who came really wanted or needed to be there, and they will talk about it with their friends, which is a SCORE!—more people talking about this work means you are making a ripple.

Being angry, annoyed or outraged can be terrific motivators. Use them. Get mad, and when it's time to build change, compose yourself and get curious. It makes more friends—allies—for your work in the long run, and you get points for being mature (as well as saves face because you didn't make up a story in your head to inaccurately assume the worst).

You Performed. Now What?

add**verb's** website will be able to host not only new material, but also your advice to other groups who will perform the pieces. It will help to know what kinds of audiences you worked with, how the pieces you performed were received, what you would recommend doing, and other discoveries you made along the way. add**verb** would like to put your feedback, links to any video of the work (as long as you're 100% sure that it is safe and permissible to put people on the internet BEFORE you post), and any MP3 files you create on the website as well. Got questions? Message us!

So, allies of the world unite and break a leg!

add**verb** Productions is thrilled to put out our first add**verb** Publication— this not-so-little book you are holding in your hands. Now, go for it. Add the verb.

Cathy Plourde
Founder/Director/Playwright
add**verb** Productions, March 2011
www.addverbproductions.org

How the Out & Allied Anthology Came to Be

add**verb** has long worked with youth to develop their own performance pieces, in addition to presenting touring productions for young adult audiences.

In 2007 the idea came to develop a youth-written collection of LGBTQ & A work that focused on cultivating allies. The bystanders, the masses in the middle, are the ones who need to be advocates alongside their LGBTQ friends and family. Slowly the project moved along, almost entirely with the stewardship of young volunteers and interns: Tess, Devon and Jen, Vanessa and Andrew, Sophia and Micah, and then, along came Emmy to put the project over the finish line.

add**verb** used a variety of strategies to generate new material and encourage submissions: workshops with LGBTQ youth, presentations to GSA's, an all-call via national email networks. With just a few exceptions the writers were between the ages of 11 and 24. It was powerful to watch an 11 year old and a 23 year old (both of whom have pieces in the book) give each other useful feedback on their drafts during a writing workshop. It was moving to get a submission in the mail from a young person in Texas who wished his school would do more. It was heartbreaking to get pieces that were clearly autobiographical with no happy ending. While still a pile of un-edited scripts, the project was featured on MTV's Think site (thanks, Jaime) and won Best Youth Program from Maine's League of Young Voters.

So, without further ado…

Out & Allied Anthology

Proud
by Lauren Kidd

I stand tall
Shoulders back
In perfect posture
I walk outside with a smile on my face
Rain and clouds can't break this feeling away
I am happy.
I am proud.

I'm fully aware of what's ahead of me
What I could fall into
What I could be
I don't care
I am happy.
I am proud.

They are all so curious of what brings this smile to my face
I got into an argument with my best friend
My parents are fighting
I don't even have a job
Even the weather's bad
But I don't care
I am happy.
I am proud.

They all just don't understand
They criticize because what they see
Isn't supposed to be allowed
Well they need to get used to it
Because I am here
Standing tall
Shoulders back
In perfect posture
And most importantly
I am proud.

I'm proud to say that when I see her
The butterflies in my stomach seem to fly
I'm proud to say that when I see her
Everything in the world freezes in time
I'm proud to say that when I see her
It makes me want to be a better person
A better woman
Just for her

Because I woke up this morning smiling
Because I know in this destruction and wreck
Aside from all the secrets being kept
As well as all the things that may be said
In addition to the way we get looked at
I know today I'll see her
And I'm proud to say
That's all that matters to me.

Understand
by Anonymous Youth Artists Team

CHARACTERS:
THREE ACTORS

1: Hey!
2: Why don't
3: People
1: You
2: Me
3: We
ALL: Not understand?

(For each of the sections, the actors step forward and center for their "understand" line, each time in a different pose, with a different meaning. Actors should be careful to have each saying of the word "understand" have a different "meaning" or intention for the word.)

1: Understand
2: Understand
3: Understand

(Two of the actors have positioned themselves center, shoulder to shoulder.)

1: On the first day of class, someone walked in and said—

(Other actor steps from behind, pushing between the two.)

2: I heard this teacher's a huge dyke!

(All shift their physical response, as appropriate to character, and exchange looks.)

3: Understand
1: Understand
2: Understand

(Slide into a standing pose, in a car, with driver holding wheel, another pointing ahead, and the third leaning between as though from the back seat.)

3: We were sitting in traffic when s/he pointed to the rainbow bumper sticker ahead and said—

1: What I don't get is why they have to flaunt their *gayness.* I mean you don't see straight people doing that.

(All shift their physical response, as appropriate to character, and exchange looks.)

2: Understand
3: Understand
1: Understand

(Slide into a new pose, one holding a newspaper open, another looking over at the article, another nearby.)

2: A classmate was reading a newspaper story about a hate crime and said—

3: Look at what that boy is wearing—he must have enjoyed getting beaten.

(They adjust their physical response, according to character, and exchange looks.)

1: Understand
2: Understand
3: Understand

(Shift into final pose.)

1:Why can't
2: People
3: You
1: Me
2: We
ALL: Understand?

STAGING SUGGESTIONS:
"Understand" is intended for three actors, but feel free to restage and reassign lines to fit the number of actors you want to use. We suggest that the actors speak in a repeated order, making it easier for both the actors and the audience to follow. Here we have the lines rotating 1-2-3, and changing who starts each section.

Here's how the original actors staged the piece: Enter from the side in single file, stopping in a line. When all three have arrived in place, face center. The first actor begins with a loud punctuated shout. They circle each other, stepping forward for lines. This helps slow the pace, and lets the audience really feel the power of the words and images. Note that this scene was developed to reflect real things that were said to real people. Lines can be changed to reflect a local event. Be careful to consider the impact on the audience with what you offer—do no harm!

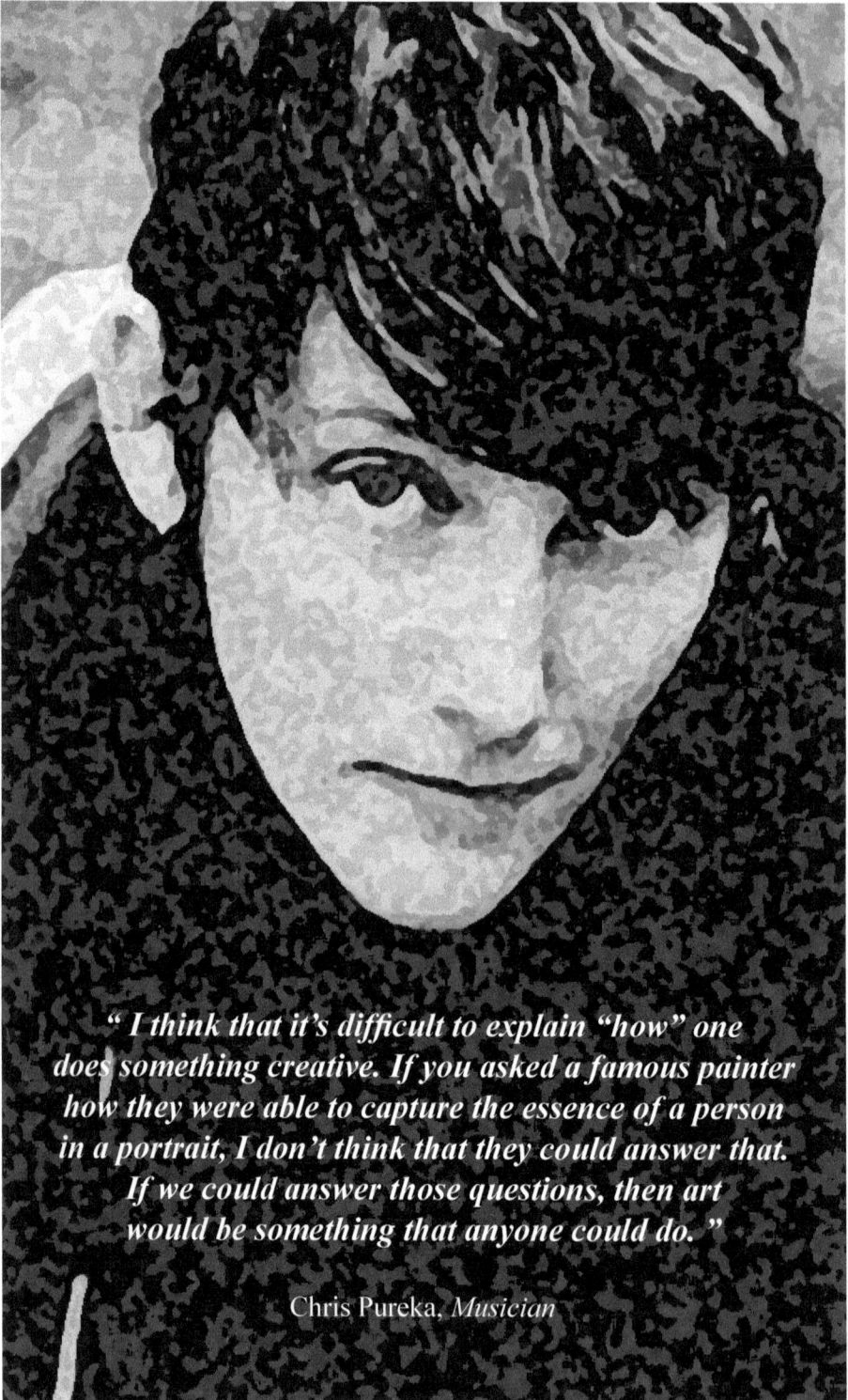

" I think that it's difficult to explain "how" one does something creative. If you asked a famous painter how they were able to capture the essence of a person in a portrait, I don't think that they could answer that. If we could answer those questions, then art would be something that anyone could do. "

Chris Pureka, *Musician*

A Phone Call
by Rai Silverstein

(ANDREW is sitting at his desk in his house. He is working diligently until the phone next to him rings and he answers it.)

ANDREW: Hello?

(Beat)

ANDREW: Hey! How are you?

(Beat)

ANDREW: Well, I have to work to do, but otherwise, I'm good. Oh hey, how did the interview go today?

(Beat)

ANDREW: That's great! So, are you coming home soon?

(Beat)

ANDREW: Oh, that's right…you have to go shopping. I forgot how little food we have.

(Beat)

ANDREW: *(Smiling)* I am not a workaholic.

(Beat)

ANDREW: I'm not! I just…have a lot of work to do. Speaking of which, I have a lot to get done today. If you want to talk tonight, you'd better let me know.

(Beat)

ANDREW: Of course I wouldn't choose work over you! Why do you think I want to get it all done before you come home?

(Beat)

ANDREW: No, it's okay. You don't have to apologize. But I really need to get this done, so I have to go now.

(Beat)

ANDREW: I love you too. Goodbye, Richard.

(Beat)

(ANDREW hangs up the phone before going back to working diligently.)

STAGING SUGGESTIONS:
The surprise is gentle and lovely in this piece. It could easily be followed by a series of images of different types of families and couples—race, ethnicity, orientation—and would serve well for a discussion about what a family looks like.

" add**verb** *is changing lives and changing the world. I wish I'd had something like this in high school.* "

T. G., *18, American University, GLSEN Northern VA*

Throwing
by Joan Lipkin and the Apple Pie ensemble, created under the auspices of That Uppity Theatre Company

CHARACTERS:

JEREMIE	DREAM
ALEX	DAN
CHRIS	SAM

JEREMIE: *(As if holding imaginary ball)* People throw all kinds of things. *(Mimes throwing ball to ALEX)*

ALEX: *(Mimes catching imaginary ball)* People throw balls. *(Mimes throwing ball to CHRIS)*

CHRIS: *(Catches imaginary ball)* People throw parties. *(Mimes festively throwing ball to DREAM)*

DREAM: *(Holding imaginary ball under one arm and throwing a kiss with the other hand)* People throw kisses. *(Mimes throwing ball to DAN)*

DAN: *(Catches imaginary ball)* People throw the trash out. *(Mimes throwing ball underhand to SAM with a big gesture)*

SAM: *(Catches imaginary ball)* People throw around ideas. *(Mimes throwing ball to JEREMIE)*

JEREMIE: *(As if holding imaginary ball)* People throw out the old for the new. *(Mimes throwing ball over his shoulder to CHRIS)*

CHRIS: *(Stretching to catch imaginary ball)* People throw together a meal. *(Mimes throwing ball to ALEX)*

ALEX: *(Mimes catching imaginary ball)* People throw horseshoes. *(Mimes throwing ball to DREAM like a horseshoe)*

DREAM: *(Mimes catching imaginary ball)* People throw ashes into the ocean. *(Pauses, mimes throwing ball to SAM)*

SAM: *(As if catching imaginary ball, winces)* People throw rotten tomatoes. *(Mimes throwing ball to JEREMIE)*

JEREMIE: *(Mimes catching imaginary ball)* People throw up. *(Mimes throwing ball to CHRIS)*

CHRIS: *(Mimes catching imaginary ball)* People throw a tantrum. *(Mimes throwing ball to DAN)*

DAN: *(Catches imaginary ball)* Fists. *(Mimes throwing ball to ALEX)*

ALEX: *(Catches imaginary ball)* Books. *(Mimes throwing ball to CHRIS)*

CHRIS: *(Catches imaginary ball)* Shoes. *(Mimes throwing ball to JEREMIE)*

JEREMIE: *(Catches imaginary ball)* Pens. *(Mimes throwing ball to DREAM)*

DREAM: *(Catches imaginary ball)* One time I was in class just sitting there doing my assignment and a bottle of baby lotion was thrown at my head. *(Rolls imaginary ball off stage)* It left a big red mark on my face. I felt my cheek and there was lotion on it *(Beat)* so I took advantage of it and rubbed it in. It felt quite soft. I just put the bottle down and started to do my work like nothing happened because in my mind, the throwers have no meaning, no matter. Just something that is there but you just don't care enough-to care. At least you try not to. A little bit after that, a pen was thrown at me. They totally missed. So that made it kinda funny. Kinda. It was not the first time something was thrown at me in that class.

SAM: Where was the teacher?

DREAM: One time, me and a couple of my friends...CHRIS was with me...

(CHRIS steps up beside DREAM.)

CHRIS: Hey. *(To audience)* That would be me.

DREAM:...were walking home from school and, out of nowhere, a plastic bag of old tuna was thrown at us. The bag exploded and splattered everywhere.

CHRIS: All we did was laugh and make jokes about how we looked covered in chopped up fish. We decided to become vegetarians. At least, for the next day.

DREAM: As many times as something like this has happened, this was the smelliest.

SAM: Where was the teacher?

CHRIS: The throwing of the tuna was actually the big finale around the end of seventh grade. A lot of things have been thrown at me. To name a few: door hinges . . .

DREAM: Tuna . . .

CHRIS: Rocks, nails . . .

DREAM: Bolts, paper wads . . .

CHRIS: Sporks, books, pens . . .

DREAM: Pencils, orange peels, bananas . . .

CHRIS: And probably countless other items.

DREAM: Yeah.

CHRIS: Yeah. Most of that list was from walking home from school. The day before the person on the bus threw the tuna, they threw a door hinge.

SAM: Where was the bus driver?!

(CHRIS and DREAM turn to the group behind them and step back.)

DAN: I've been there. I've done that. I've taken this and I've taken that. I wasn't openly gay, but they still gave it to me. Filling me up with emotion until I practically had it pouring out of my mouth. I became a fountain. A fountain of hatred, a fountain of oppression. But still spewing out excuses like, "It's all in good fun," "They don't mean anything by it…"

Was I openly gay? No, but did people still harass me for being who I was? Yes. And I don't know why. Were they afraid? Afraid of the unknown? Or different ideas? I don't know.

SAM: So, why did you want to come out?

DAN: Ask me that question in 50 years from now.

JEREMIE: It's a shame, is an easy thing to say. Oh, it's a shame that violence still persists against children in our community. Oh, it's a pity that we can't be more accepting of others. But it's more than just a shame. We are all supposed to help one another and love one another and yet here we are in 20_ _, throwing rotten fish out the window at innocent kids. Where are we? What is this? No one is concerned with the issues until someone gets hurt. Then people—well, *some* people—stand up and listen to violence, but why does it have to come to that? Why can't it be enough that someone feels threatened? Or even that they are discriminated against at all?

SAM: Where was the teacher?

ALEX: Well, it just happened once to me.

CHRIS: *This* year.

ALEX: I was in school, late for a class, running up the stairs. A can of soda fell from the top stair onto my head. It did really physically hurt, but what was really hurting me was the idea I had in my head. That my gayness is the reason that I am bothered. I think it over and over in my head. Sometimes it makes me really sad. I get depressed. And my new shirt was ruined with sticky soda. And I really liked that shirt. I felt that I don't belong. I felt maybe just by being, I am bothering others … just by being who I am. I *dream* of going away. So far away, that no one has ever been there, but I will be happy.

DREAM: Just because I am gay, people think I will just sit there and watch this stuff happen which is NOT TRUE. I want to take a stand. Not just for me but for everyone who is someone that they aren't like. Just because someone is different, they think they have the upper hand which is not true. It's not just gays or trans, it is for anyone who isn't like "them," who does not "fit in."

SAM: Yes. But where was the teacher?

ALL: Where is the teacher?

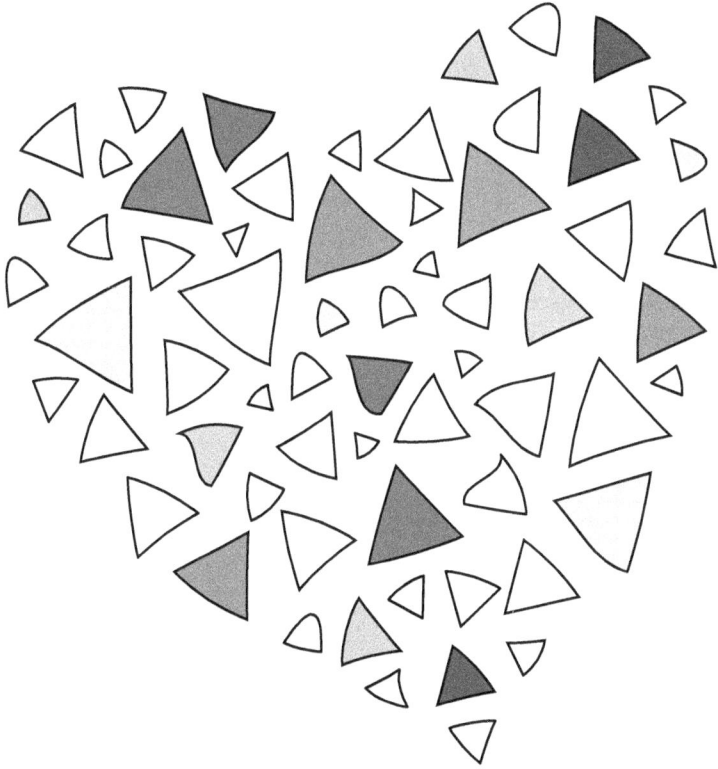

" I want the audience to feel something because doing this has been an experience that has changed me. "

Out & Allied Actor

The Crayola Crusade
by John Coons

The first time I saw a gray brick,
I knew precisely what I had to do.

My pudgy five year old fingers
plunged
into the crayon box,
rooting for a red
and were determined to set things right.

Nothing was ever broken…it was just colored the wrong way.

I didn't blame God for my new crusade,
my quest to BRICK RED conquer the concrete,
to GREEN GRASS govern the wheat fields,
to BARK BROWN bully the birches,
to SKY BLUE subdue the rainy days.

Clearly, to my superior five year intellect,
He had just forgotten.

Armed with cannons of Crayola,
I knew that the world would soon be
Picture book perfect.

Of course, it came as quite a shock
when I found out
He had not adorned me with
the popular palate.

How I longed to be colored
IN CROWD PERIWINKLE
or DUMB JOCK APRICOT
or DATING THE CHEERLEADER LAVENDER
instead of
GEEK MAUVE
AWKWARD NEON GREEN
and OH SO LONELY BLUE.

But the worst,
the most painful discovery
was when I discovered
that God had colored my heart
the wrong way.

You see, with all the
ROMAN CATHOLIC MAROON
and
SPARKLING FAMILY VALUES WHITE,
there was no room,

none,

for HOMOSEXUAL PEA SOUP GREEN.

Wrapped in wax garments,
I colored myself,
covered myself,
in 8-COLOR masks
and Yellow Cardboard Box Armor—
and my tears were
BITTER AZURE
and
GOD BLAMING TURQUOISE.

" *We're better off
for all that we let in.* "

Indigo Girls, *Musicians*

I was surrounded by nonbrown birches
greenless wheat
cloudy skies
and anchored within,
a heavy Gray Brick
in the pit
of my stomach.

My last thought scribbled away in my mind
as I hit the gritty pavement,
and the box slipped from my fingers
and scattered around me in a halo of spear shaped shades,

"If only I had a
       single
            red
                  crayon."

Wishes
by Bells

CHARACTERS:
FIRST GIRL
SECOND GIRL

SETTING: A hallway in a school.

NOTE:
Dialogue is between FIRST GIRL and SECOND GIRL unless indicated otherwise.

(Both girls are talking to friends walking down a hall. They stop at lockers across from each other and turn to face one another. Their friends keep talking to them.)

(Conversation stops.)

FIRST GIRL: *(To audience)* The hurt I feel in my heart when I watch her move through her everyday life. The longing for her to notice me, and look at me with those beautiful eyes. And I wish…

SECOND GIRL: *(To friend)*…she'd even glance my way.

FIRST GIRL: *(To self)* I wonder if she's thinking about me.

SECOND GIRL: *(To self)* Did she just look at me?

BOTH: Yes.

SECOND GIRL: *(To audience)* But she's not like me. She doesn't know how it feels to have to watch and listen and to pretend the world is perfect and that Dad accepts me…and she loves me back.

FIRST GIRL: *(To audience)* What if she felt the same way? What if…

SECOND GIRL: *(To self)*…She really did? Even then…

FIRST GIRL: *(Let down)*…It wouldn't work…

SECOND GIRL:…Because of…

FIRST GIRL:…Her dad…

BOTH:…and our feared hope of being out.

SECOND GIRL: I'm sorry.

FIRST GIRL: *(Pleading)* I wish…

SECOND GIRL:…I know. I do too.

FIRST GIRL: But I can…

SECOND GIRL:…Still pretend.

BOTH: *(To audience)* Right?

STAGING SUGGESTIONS:
Lockers can be pantomimed with actors facing front. If working with an ensemble, other actors can create a soundscape to open and close scene.

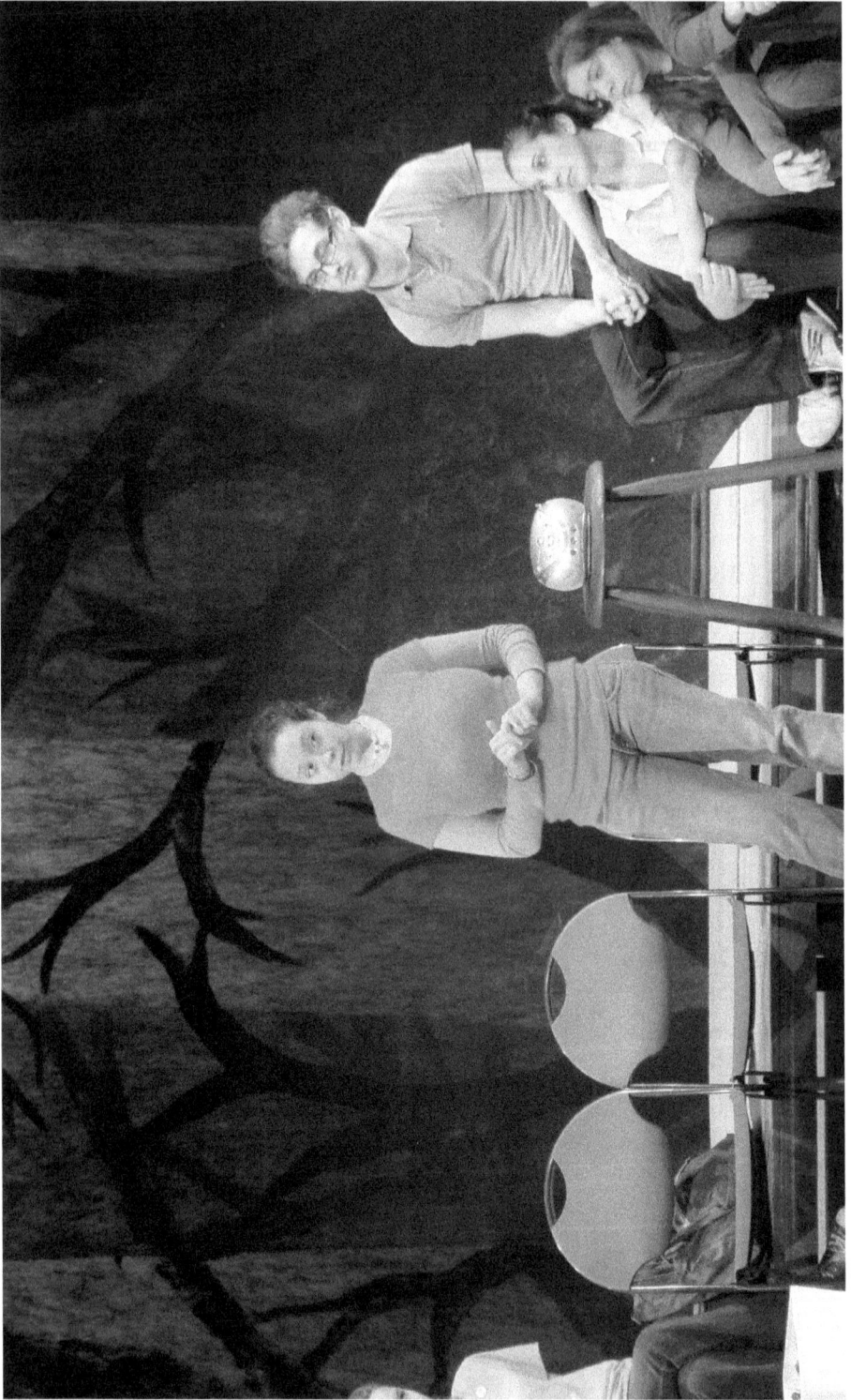

Our Uttermost Important Gift
by Kayla Cowan

Two girls in friendship
"how cute?"
two girls in love
"blasphemy!"

This muse could kill me
so just in case
say you'll take the trip with me
look to the stars
as your hands lock with mine.

Our parachute heart
knots our insides
even this piercing light
couldn't blind me from your stare
with one last breath
I say goodnight
with one last breath
the world gasps
at a love so bright.

I tell her,
don't cry
don't fret
our love is much too bright
much too vast
for others to get
I tell her,
even I almost lose it
even I fear the next morning
facing the world,
facing myself.

All I did was dream love
all I did was reminisce love
now that I have her
I no longer survive,
I live.

Slowly,
the good in me shines
slowly,
the beauty in me blooms.

Held by her,
I let go.

From up here we are safe
from up here we are beautiful
gliding below a complete heart
we take the risk
the risk of sharing
sharing ourselves—with each other
sharing ourselves—with the world.

Proving our uttermost important gift
a love we grow in ourselves
only to carry to a soul
who wandered aimlessly and alone
secretly holding us
in our dark moments of despair.

Air is what we breathe
emptiness is what we take in
Love,
is what we scramble for
whom no one is exempt of
nor less deserving
once held,
love lives within—eternally.

Rationalizing
by Shawna Searles

Men are from Mars.
Women are from Venus.

So I guess it only makes sense that once in awhile someone's gonna want someone from their own planet. Martian to Martian, Venusian to Venusian, it only makes sense. I mean, who really wants to date someone who speaks a whole 'nother tongue, right?

Right.

So it only makes sense that if a girl is from Venus, after awhile she's going to get sick of trying to translate Martian, and go back to the planet where they speak her language.

Right?
Right.

So, then it's not my fault. It's not my fault that she went back to Venus, right? Not my fault that I was the last Martian she saw.

But that doesn't mean I don't get blamed, you know? Most of it's just teasing—me being so bad that I ruined her for other guys—so bad that it made her go lesbo. But that's the guys. I knew it was a joke. We all did. But that didn't mean it didn't hurt a little. I really liked her. I liked her a lot. And I probably would have gotten over it faster if it wasn't for her mother.

Her mother is one of those women who could've walked right out of the Bible. A loyal Eve, who despite her past transgressions, fell away in the wake of her now staunch and steadfast loyalty to the word of God. She expected no less from her daughter. When I saw them both at church, I waved. No hard feelings, it meant. Her mother didn't think so. She glared at me.

It meant, "job well done" to her. She didn't see an ex-boyfriend in me. I could hear exactly what she saw as clearly as if she had spoken it. "Oh look," she glared, "there's the boy who made my daughter a dyke. There's the reason my little girl's going to burn in Hell."

But it's not my fault. She just doesn't like guys, that's all. Right? Right. It's not a choice. I've done my research. I've checked it out. It can't be my fault. It just doesn't work that way. She likes girls. So what? I can respect that. I can understand that.

Right?
Right.

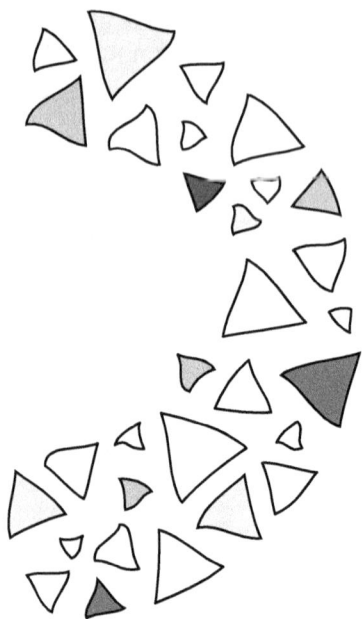

" I am doing this for my brother, my mother, doing it for my family... what makes this performance so unique is that it shows the diversity within diversity, it encompasses so much more than just being 'gay.' "

Out & Allied Actor

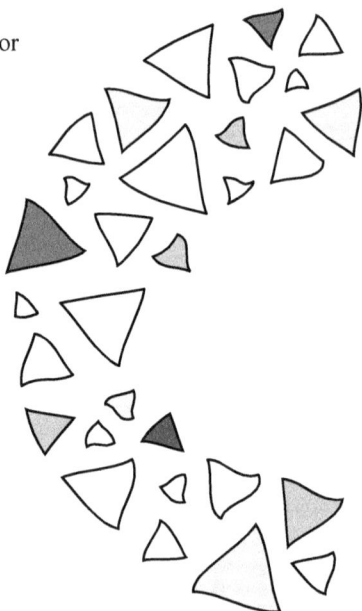

The Straightest Gay Man in the World
by Micah Malenfant

CHARACTERS:
ABE, a charismatic, outgoing guy.
TRAVIS, a dude.
ERIC, another guy, who is gay.

SETTING: ABE, TRAVIS, and ERIC are sitting at a table. The table could be at different locations depending on the audience. For example: for a college-aged audience the setting could be a bar, for a high school or middle school audience the setting could be a local hangout like a pizza parlor.

(Lights up on ABE, TRAVIS, and ERIC sitting at a table.)

ABE: I can't believe you said you were quitting the team two weeks ago.

TRAVIS: Coach Scott was pissing me off.

ABE: I was so scared you were serious.

TRAVIS: I was serious.

ERIC: But you love rugby.

TRAVIS: I hate Coach more than I love rugby.

ABE: But we all love you.

TRAVIS: Thanks…I guess...

ERIC: What bothered you so much?

TRAVIS: He always says I'm soft and I'm too worried about re-injuring my knee.

ERIC: It's been awhile since you hurt your knee. Aren't you fine now?

TRAVIS: Yeah and I'm not worried about it.

ABE: Well it's just…sometimes you seem a bit hesitant.

TRAVIS: Maybe I am, but he doesn't need to make those "gay" jokes all the time.

ABE: He makes those jokes about everyone.

ERIC: Yeah, it's just the way he is. He doesn't know any better.

TRAVIS: It's just some of the things he says just really get to me. I mean, if a school official heard some of the remarks he makes at practice, he'd be fired in a heartbeat.

ABE: But he's a good coach. We need him.

TRAVIS: Well there's no excuse for some of the things he says.

ERIC: You're right.

ABE: *(Looking at a text message on his cell phone)* Well I'd love to stay and chat, but the lady's waiting for me. See ya tomorrow. I'm glad you're back, Travis.

(ABE gets up and hugs TRAVIS from behind. TRAVIS shrugs his shoulders to try to get ABE off of him. After ABE has left TRAVIS looks over his shoulder to make sure he is gone.)

TRAVIS: Man, he is the gayest straight kid I know.

ERIC: How do you know he's straight?

TRAVIS: He has a girlfriend.

ERIC: That doesn't necessarily mean he's straight.

TRAVIS: Well he's the king of man hugs and I could swear he's tried to kiss me a few times.

ERIC: *(Laughs)* That's just Abe.

TRAVIS: Oh…

ERIC: What?

TRAVIS: Nothing.

ERIC: What?

TRAVIS: It's just, I always forget that you're gay.

ERIC: Haha, it's fine.

TRAVIS: I mean it's just so weird 'cause you act so straight. I mean Abe's the gayest straight kid I know and you gotta admit you must be the straightest gay kid in the world.

ERIC: Well…I don't really get how you can be gay and straight unless you're bisexual.

TRAVIS: You know what I mean.

ERIC: Explain…

TRAVIS: I mean, you're just one of the guys. You're on the rugby team, a mountain biker, an outdoorsman, and you like to hang out with the guys.

ERIC: So?

TRAVIS: Well, I wouldn't expect a gay guy to be able to say he spent half of last summer camping in the woods of Maine.

ERIC: Then what would you expect a gay guy to do?

TRAVIS: I don't know…Spend half his summer shopping? Work at Abercrombie and Fitch? Have tons of friends that are girls and hardly any that are dudes?

ERIC: *(Laughs)* Not every gay guy is like that.

TRAVIS: Sure…I guess.

ERIC: I mean, everyone has their own unique personality whether they are gay or straight.

TRAVIS: Yeah but it's just really strange.

ERIC: Why?

TRAVIS: I mean usually I can walk right into a room and spot everyone who is gay within my first glance.

ERIC: So you got gay-dar?

TRAVIS: Exactly.

ERIC: Well, it's not that simple all the time. *(Beat)* I'll tell you what…

TRAVIS: Yeah?

ERIC: Tomorrow I'll go see Coach Scott and tell him not to bother you anymore and not to make any more "gay" jokes.

TRAVIS: Thanks man.

(Lights)

Dining Out
by Vianca Yohn

CHARACTERS:

GENTLEMAN	WAITRESS 1
LADY	WAITRESS 2
BOY	MAN 1
GIRL	MAN 2

SETTING: Romantic, candle-lit bistro in late 1950's America.

NOTES: Neither MAN 1 or MAN 2 should speak out loud but should only carry on a silent conversation. The WAITRESS 1 and WAITRESS 2 should practically be mirror images, always speaking and moving in unison. ALL refers to GENTELMAN, LADY, BOY, and GIRL.

(Lights up on three tables onstage: one SL, one CS, and one SR. GENTLEMAN and LADY are seated at SR table; BOY and GIRL are seated at SL table; MAN 1 and MAN 2 are seated at CS table.)

GENTLEMAN: They're perfectly fine, cigars. I don't see all the fuss. Those left-wing liberal loonies don't know what they're talking about.

LADY: Well, yes, darling; cigars are fine. It's cigarettes they want to get rid of.

GENTLEMAN: Is it?

GIRL: It is! It's totally true!

BOY: *(Uninterested)* I never would have guessed…

GIRL: I know! Isn't it incredible?

BOY: It sure is.

LADY: Is what?

GENTLEMAN: Cigarettes. The liberals are looking to outlaw cigarettes?

LADY: Oh, I suppose so. They're always trying to ban this, that, or the other.

BOY: How did you find out?

(GIRL leans over and whispers into BOY's ear.)

GENTLEMAN: You shouldn't do that, you know.

BOY: What?

(GIRL resumes whispering.)

LADY: What?

GENTLEMAN: Speak ill of people, that's what.

BOY and LADY: But—

(GIRL yanks BOY back to her and continues whispering.)

GENTLEMAN: Everyone is entitled to his or her own opinions.

LADY: *(Indignantly)* You only say that because they're not trying to illegalize cigars.

(WAITRESS 1 enters SR and addresses GENTLEMAN and LADY; WAITRESS 2 enters SL and addresses BOY and GIRL. Neither WAITRESS pays any mind to the MEN.)

WAITRESSES: Good evening. What can I get you to drink tonight?

LADY: Water.

GENTLEMAN: Water.

" *Life is too important
to be taken seriously!* "

Oscar Wilde, *Playwright*

GIRL: Water.

BOY: Water.

ALL:…please.

(WAITRESSES exit)

GENTLEMAN and BOY: Well.

LADY and GIRL: "Well" what?

GENTLEMAN and BOY: What?

LADY and GIRL: Well?

GENTLEMAN and BOY: Oh!

(BOY leans toward GIRL, and they whisper to each other.)

GENTLEMAN: Yes, yes, as I was saying—

GIRL: What?

GENTLEMAN:—about opinions. Or was it cigars?

(WAITRESSES enter as before and set water on tables.)

ALL: Thank you.

WAITRESSES: You're welcome. Now, what would you like to order.

LADY: Hm?

GENTLEMAN: Huh?

BOY: What?

GIRL: Oh…

ALL: Give us a minute.

(WAITRESSES exit. ALL sigh, then pick up menus.)

LADY: Hm…

GENTLEMAN: Huh…

BOY: What about—

GIRL: Oh!

LADY and GIRL: Chicken marsala!

BOY and GIRL: Surf and turf!

BOY and GENTLEMAN: Vegetable lasagna!

GENTLEMAN and LADY: Shrimp and crawfish linguini!

LADY: Which shall we order?

BOY: Let's get spaghetti.

GIRL: I don't want spaghetti.

GENTLEMAN: How about filet minon?

LADY: Oh, that's too much.

GIRL: Let's get spaghetti.

BOY: All right, that sounds good.

LADY: I want filet minon.

GENTLEMAN: Splendid choice, dear.

(WAITRESSES enter as before.)

GENTLEMAN: We'll both have the filet minon.

BOY: We'll both have the spaghetti.

(WAITRESSES write down orders.)

WAITRESSES: And which salad would you like—house, or Caesar?

(GENTLEMAN and LADY exchange glances; BOY and GIRL do the same. GENTLEMAN and BOY both shrug as LADY and GIRL sit back and stay silent.)

GENTLEMAN: Caesar.

BOY: House.

(WAITRESSES write down orders. They glance at CS then at each other. The MEN gesture to the WAITRESSES, but they turn and exit instead. MEN glance at each other, obviously upset.)

GENTLEMAN: Service is a little slow, isn't it?

BOY: I wonder what took the waitresses so long to get to us.

LADY and GIRL: Better late than never.

(As the above exchange is taking place, MAN 2 is patting MAN 1's hand in a gesture of comfort. The two MEN move closer together, taking each other's hands. LADY and GIRL simultaneously notice MEN and lean forward to whisper to GENTLEMAN and BOY, respectively. LADY and GIRL gesture to MEN. GENTLEMAN and BOY look at MEN, then turn back to LADY and GIRL, all in unison.)

GENTLEMAN: Unacceptable—

BOY: Unbelievable—

GIRL: If that's what they want to do—

LADY: Don't be a gossip—

(WAITRESSES enter with salads as MEN kiss.)

WAITRESSES: Oh!

GIRL: Awww!

LADY: My word!

(GENTLEMAN and BOY stand abruptly and in unison, slamming their palms on the table.)

GENTLEMAN and BOY: We're leaving!

(Lights)

For the Rest of My Life
by Andrew Cole

CHARACTERS:
MOM
SON

NOTE:
Lines should flow together as if one person were talking.

MOM: I will remember that night

SON: for the rest of my life. I'd been thinking about how that conversation would happen. Could I do it? Would she understand? Did she already know? I never quite knew how I would start this talk, but I had always thought my uncle was gay, so I figured I'd start by asking my mom about her

MOM: brother who was gay. We were from rural Downeast Maine, and being gay just wasn't an option. He got married and had two kids. After a few years, they got separated. Shortly after, he moved in with his roommate and he stayed single

SON: for the rest of his life. When he was 46 he was diagnosed with cancer. The doctors found it late and gave him only a few months to live. I was in middle school when he got sick and all I really remember is my mother going back and forth between Maine

MOM: and Massachusetts almost every weekend for over a year. My brother was a fighter and lived much longer than the doctors anticipated. As time went on, he couldn't fight anymore. A few nights before my brother died, I was

SON: sitting in his room with him. His roommate definitely had a drinking problem and that night, like most, he was drunk by 8:00. In his drunken stupor, my uncle's roommate started yelling at him in front of my mother and all of my other uncles: "YOU NEVER LOVED ME"

MOM: "WHY DIDN'T YOU TELL THEM ABOUT US?" And just like that, my brother, my dying brother, was outed by his drunken asshole boyfriend. I could see the anger, hurt, and sadness in my brother's eyes. He tried to hide that he was upset

SON: but my uncle, my mother's oldest brother, stayed strong until the moment he died. My uncle lived his entire life in the closet and I knew after hearing this story, I needed to tell my mom. I needed to tell her

MOM: that he was gay. My son needed to be able to live as himself, and not have to live a lie like my brother. I had always thought I knew that he was gay. Finally, at almost 17 years old, he finally came to me to tell me

SON: that I was gay. That was the scariest, bravest, and most proud night of my life and I will remember it

MOM: for the rest of my life.

EDITOR'S NOTE:

Poems are great ensemble pieces—often good
for opening, closing or transitioning between pieces.
They could also establish a theme throughout the show.

Erin
by Elizabeth Peek/Wykes

While you're sleeping,
I watch your chest rise and fall.
I still feel nervous around you
Despite the fact you're not awake.
I want to reach over and touch your face
To make sure that you aren't an illusion
But I can't. I won't allow myself to.

You would never like me anyway.
You like boys just the way I like girls:
Anti-Society, dressed in edgy clothes, musically inclined.
I go both directions while you only go one.

I get up and walk over to your couch,
And collapse on the cushions into another restless sleep.

It's been almost five years since I last slept by you.
It's been almost four months since I last saw you.
You have become even more beautiful.
You have gone even farther away from me.

STAGING SUGGESTIONS:
Casting is flexible for individual, multiple actors or ensemble. Can use one actor for straight forward delivery, or get creative! Multiple actors could take places in various parts of the room/stage and have assigned lines or sections from the piece. Perhaps actors repeat their sequence multiple times, overlapping, or call-and-response. Clue the audience in to where to look (especially if only cycling through the piece once) as they will spend more time trying to find where the voice is coming from than hearing the words.

Use of slides or images with either live or recorded voices could also be interesting.

After Breakfast
by Meghan Brodie

CHARACTERS:
MOM, a woman in her forties.
DAD, a man in his forties.
RACHAEL, a young woman in her late teens.

SETTING: A kitchen table, Saturday morning. DAD is working on his laptop and MOM is reading the newspaper. The remains of breakfast are on the table.

(RACHAEL enters.)

MOM: You want some breakfast? Or since it is almost noon, maybe lunch?

RACHAEL: *(Getting some juice)* Not yet.

MOM: We're going to pick Beth up at the airport in a couple of hours. Do you want to come?

RACHAEL: I'm going out later so maybe not.

MOM: We might go straight to dinner—do you want to meet us?

RACHAEL: I sort of already have dinner plans.

MOM: With who?

RACHAEL: *(Hesitates)* With this person I met.

MOM: "This person?"

RACHAEL: At the coffee shop. With this girl I met at the coffee shop.

MOM : Oh, okay fine. Then we'll see you later tonight when we get back.

RACHAEL: Yeah...Actually, I sort of wanted to tell you something.

(MOM and DAD both look at her.)

RACHAEL: It's a date.

MOM: The dinner with the coffee shop girl?

RACHAEL: Yeah.

MOM: Oh. *(Looks at DAD)*

DAD: Does she ride a motorcycle?

RACHAEL: Um, no.

DAD: Does she have a record?

RACHAEL: Not that I know of.

DAD: Is she older than I am?

RACHAEL: Ew. No.

DAD: Okay, well have fun.

RACHAEL: That's it?

DAD: What? Is there something else I should be asking?

RACHAEL: No. No. No at all.

MOM: Hold on. So now you're gay?

RACHAEL: Mom.

MOM: You were dating boys and now you're dating a girl.

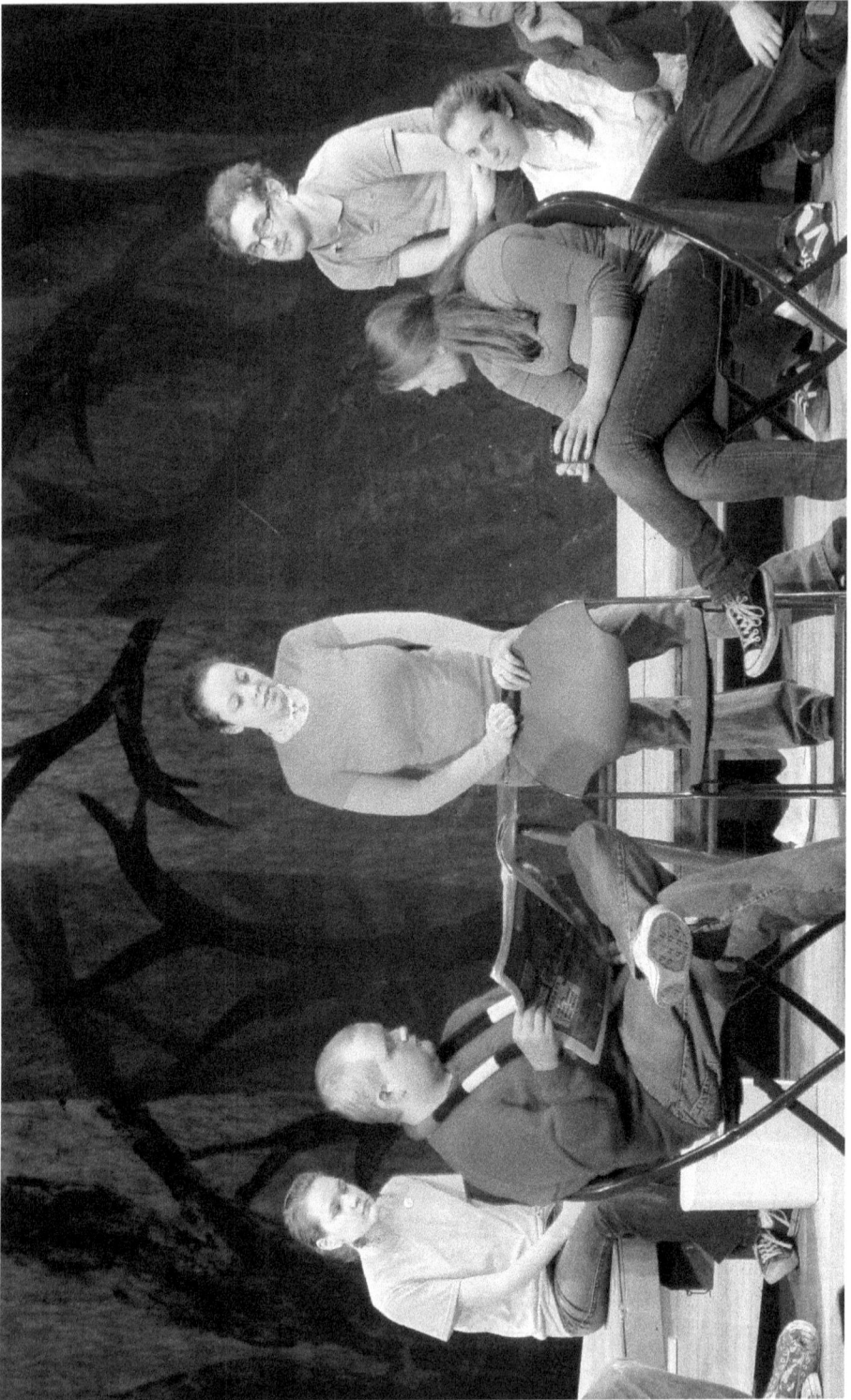

RACHAEL: First of all, I'm not dating a girl; I'm going on *a* date with a girl. And going on a date with a girl doesn't make me gay.

MOM: So what does it make you?

RACHAEL: I don't know. It doesn't make me anything. Why does it have to make me something?

MOM: Well it's something, right?

RACHAEL: Fine. Go with bisexual, if you need a word. But this is silly.

MOM: Okay, I get gay and straight, but if you're bisexual, you eventually end up with someone which would then make you either gay or straight.

RACHAEL: Not really. You can like both boys and girls and just end up with one or the other. You're just open to both. Think about it like this: straight means you want to end up with someone of the opposite sex, gay means you want to end up with someone of the same sex, and bisexual means it could go either way. Does that help?

MOM: So now I should say you're bisexual if someone asks?

RACHAEL: Mom, *who* is going to ask?

MOM: I don't know. What if Beth asks what you're doing tonight.

RACHAEL: Just tell her I'm on a date.

MOM: But what if she asks for details?

RACHAEL: Um, Mom, how often do you find yourself discussing my dating life? That's just weird. It's nobody's business.

MOM: I'm not embarrassed.

RACHAEL: Nobody said you were.

MOM: *(To DAD)* And you don't have anything else to say?

DAD: Like what? She likes a girl.

MOM: You're not even a little bit surprised?

DAD: I don't know. She likes a girl. So what.

MOM: You're taking this awfully well. I mean, I am taking it well, but you—you aren't even fazed or saying anything.

DAD: I experimented a little in college. I mean who's not a little bit bi?

MOM: Excuse me?

MOM and DAD: *(Overlapping)* We'll talk about it later.

RACHAEL: I'm kind of impressed.

MOM: It's a big deal. And does this mean you don't want kids anymore? If you end up with a girl, how will you have kids?

RACHAEL: Mom, I'm going to dinner, not to Vegas to get hitched to this girl. I'm not making life decisions. And I could still have kids if I wanted—but we are *not* having that discussion. I'm just going on a date.

MOM: Okay. I'm fine with it. I love you. I just feel like we should talk about it. It's something new.

RACHAEL: What do you want to talk about?

MOM: I don't know. You just out of the blue decided you are bisexual. I just want to understand...And I don't want you to get beaten up.

RACHAEL: I am not going to get beaten up. Jesus. This really isn't a big deal. And I didn't decide I was bisexual. I like this girl and if that makes me bi, then fine.

MOM: You know I love you, right?

RACHAEL: Yes, Mom.

DAD: Ann, why don't we get ready to go. She can tell us about her date later—after she gets back from Vegas with her wife and three adopted children.

RACHAEL: Not helping.

DAD: Eat some lunch.

MOM: Alright. Well, have fun. Bring her over sometime.

DAD: Yeah. But not on a motorcycle.

RACHAEL: Ha. Ha. Still not helping.

(Lights)

" *You just have to try and do
as much as you can, and make people informed,
make people aware, and I'm very fortunate
that I'm in a position to do that.* "

Elton John, *Musician*

To The Boy Who Yelled "Faggot"
Outside Wildcatessen a Few Weeks Ago
by Marie Coyle

Hi...this is awkward. You probably don't remember me, but I was sitting outside the coffee shop a few weeks ago on a Thursday night. You walked by; I was on a bench. If this doesn't ring a bell, let me help... it was dusk. You had curly hair and a shirt with Greek letters on it. I won't try to guess which house—that wouldn't be fair.

You shouted "faggot," and there are a few things I'd like to say. First, though, could we clarify your meaning? Is it possible that you didn't mean it in a homophobic way? Could you, for example, have been referring to a small bundle of wood intended for burning? Perhaps you spotted such a bundle nearby and wanted to inform us of its presence. Or, no, maybe you wanted a cigarette and wanted to treat your neighbors to a bit of vintage Brit slang. Even still, maybe, at that precise moment, you had a craving for a meatball in pork sauce prepared in a Polish fashion. I wouldn't want to insult you by misinterpreting your intentions when shouting such a word.

Maybe I'm not incorrect. Maybe you meant it as in: "hey, gay person." This is probably more likely. Are you stuck in the stage of linguistic development where all you can do is name nouns in your vision? Bike, car, tree, queer? You saw me, you announced me—how thoughtful! Did you want to make sure I knew, you knew, what I was? Or did you just want to inform others around us who might not have noticed? Either way, thank you for your service.

It's not your fault. You've been taught that this word is okay. Every Will Farrell movie you've ever seen is thick with this word. The butt of most jokes, the classic one-liner, the ultimate insult: perfect. It's not as if anyone ever told you this word wasn't exactly kind. Your friends probably laughed and echoed you. Your parents might have pretended not to hear. Your RA might have censored you with a feeble "word choice." Useless. After all, what could you learn from that? Simply not to swear in the presence of anyone with a University Staff shirt?

I'm sorry, I apologize. I was rude. You see, I didn't respond to your direct address, which is incredibly impolite. The reason is simple and clear: I did not know how to respond! "Hey, straight?" "Hey, hetereo?" "Hey, human?" I ran into writer's block because, after all, there are so many words to describe you—but none of them carry much power. No labels I could toss your way would carry the same violence, so poetically, it wouldn't have worked.

Or should I say nothing at all? Is this our new invented politeness? To look down, feign deafness, walk faster, search the purse, check the phone, jangle the keys? To walk and keep walking and no one around you will speak up?

To The Students Around Us Who Heard: Where were you? Where the hell was your voice?!

To be quiet and polite and not respond. This is what you want from me, I know. Why else would you say that, if not to remind me that you don't want me here?

I promise: give me another word with the same weight and I will throw it back at you.

I guess most of all this letter is a request. Two requests actually, let me be selfish. First, please have some answers ready for me before you use that word again on me or any of my friends. Second, if you won't at least do that, please let it end with words and not progress to physical violence.

Say "hi" if you see me around—I'll buy you a coffee.

If I Speak
by Rob Greatness

Infants do not enter the world with the verbal skills necessary to communicate their precise wants and needs. Without regard for time, location, availability, infants unleash cries that serve as alarms for acknowledgement. The fact that they have no words to describe their discomforts does not mean these discomforts do not exist.

The fact that language and small-mindedness have not led you to understand who I am and that I am does not compromise my existence. Nor does it erase the discomfort of being invisible. In your world, I become infantile. I am small and vulnerable but my wants and needs are still immediate. You have not known me long enough to telegraph and anticipate, in order to relate to me.

You have not grown to love me, yet.

Like a baby, I might die in silence. I understand why the stereotypical Black is loud and the stereotypical Gay is flamboyant. I understand now that I must cry in order to be heard, lest I aid in the compromising of my own existence.

If I do not speak, you will not understand that I am here and that we all have infantile needs and care giving abilities that can be bridged be noticing one another.

There is no manual for humanity, but, we can create a formula to nourish ourselves and we can change what is soiled. We can protect and engage one another. We can facilitate the expulsion of each other's hot air in a gentle manner. I can give you support until you have grown enough to hold your own head up. And, in the bond that can grow between us, we can learn each other and we can learn ourselves. Perhaps then you will understand my cries and will take care to prevent them.

Perhaps you can grow to love me, if I speak.

GREY
by Mea Tavares, written at age 19

(Editor's Note: Mea's piece is more in the "performance art" genre, and we wanted to include it not only because it is powerful, but it might give you some ideas on how to think of interesting staging for some poems, use of ensemble, etc. One word of caution: make sure you are very clear with the audience what you want them to do, and when, which in turn implies that you have gotten them to agree to do it. It's best not to push an unwilling participant as that may spoil your intentions.)

SET:
Three boxes evenly spaced DS in this order: WHITE BOX, GREY BOX, BLACK BOX. These can just be cardboard boxes that are painted their respective shades. They need to be big enough to be seen and to hold clothing items.

ACTOR COSTUME:
Actor wears gender-neutral, black clothing as a base costume. Additions will be made from the WHITE BOX and BLACK BOX at different times in the piece.

WHITE BOX: "GIRL" clothes – a bandanna to be worn on the head, and a skirt

BLACK BOX: "BOY" clothes – a baseball hat and a button down collared shirt

(The ACTOR greets the audience directly, explaining their role and instructions, assigning a numbered "line" to each audience member.)

ACTOR: When I stand at the white box, those of you with the "White Box" lines please read them in unison or as moved, repeating until I leave the white box. When I stand at the black box, those with "Black Box" lines please read them in unison or as moved, repeating until I leave the black box. You *(Indicating an audience member)* can read number 1, you number 2 etc.

(ACTOR reestablishes the fourth wall through movement, sound or energy and begins scene.)

ACTOR stands at WHITE BOX and puts on contents of box. This represents "wearing" femininity. Trying it on, it doesn't fit well. Body language is accentuated attempts at femininity, all that fail. Audience reads lines that correspond with WHITE BOX all at the same time so there is a jumble of voices.

ACTOR removes feminine clothing, returning to neutral costume, and crosses stage to BLACK BOX.

ACTOR puts on contents of BLACK BOX. This represents binary transition from female to male. Still binary concept of "wearing" masculinity. This doesn't fit well either. Audience reads lines that correspond with BLACK BOX all at the same time so there is a jumble of voices.

ACTOR removes masculine clothing, returning to neutral costume, and moves center stage to GREY BOX. There is no Audience script for the GREY BOX. The result is silence.

(ACTOR exits, to end scene.)

Print two different cards, and make at least enough for each audience participation line. It is possible to print double the number of cards, and have more than one person assigned to each line. Or, conversely, if concerned about number of audience members and number of lines to be distributed, the same audience members can read for each of the box colors. These should be given out prior to the start of the piece, and with a bigger audience, assignment of lines should also be organized before the show.

WHITE BOX

1) You'd be so pretty if you grew your hair out.

2) Excuse me, but this is the LADIES room.

3) Did you shave your head because you have cancer or because you're gay?

4) Were you born a girl? Because I can't picture it.

5) I can't date you anymore. My mom found out.

6) You're in the 6th grade now. You HAVE to shave your armpits.

7) Do you think you'd be more of a girl if you weren't afraid of men?

BLACK BOX

1) How can you be a feminist and reject being a woman?

2) How can you be a boy and not want to be a Man? You have to transition. You can't stay a boy forever.

3) Real guys don't talk with their hands that much.

4) Your emotions are really girly.

5) You look like you're twelve.

6) I can't date you anymore. I need to be with a real Man.

" *Political poems are love poems,*
and then love poems can be political in this society
where people can be so separated from each other. "

Andrea Gibson, *Slam Poet*

We Fly Like Butterflies in Harmonic Symphony
by Kayla Cowan

We're born and
somehow our lives
have already been going
someone turned on the button
like a head start in a race
only the opposite

I've been pushed back
while the expectations bury me
as I fail to catch up
I shut down.
as I fail to feel loved
I fall inside.
deep into myself
until I'm unrecognizable
to me, to them, to everyone

No longer a boy, no longer a human
I am a shell
like an ice sculpture
I pretend to be art
in the process of beauty
in the process of becoming

A true escape
to a scene with the others
like me—they're displaced
intricate beauties
overflowing with love

Cut us open
we just might take it
"Do our parts match?"
"Do our faces horrify you?"
Quit staring
open us up already
as you "tower"—claiming your "significance"

Keep your pedestals
don't dare come down
look, up in the sky
a thousand precious butterflies
in place of pain, hate
our shunned souls
grew wings

Watch as we grow
into something greater
than your small minds can comprehend
listen if you will
for we transition
in harmonic symphony

With constant disturbance
with constant doubt
the long, hard road
begins to crack, begins to crumble
before I fall into deep depression
before I'm caught in my web of misery
I must break free
the sun is hot
as I unzip my cocoon

I never knew beauty
until I witnessed my wings
I never knew myself
until I witnessed myself, my true self
old skin, old thoughts, old friends are left behind

We're born and
somehow our life
has already been going
I turned on the button
like a head start in a race
I caught up

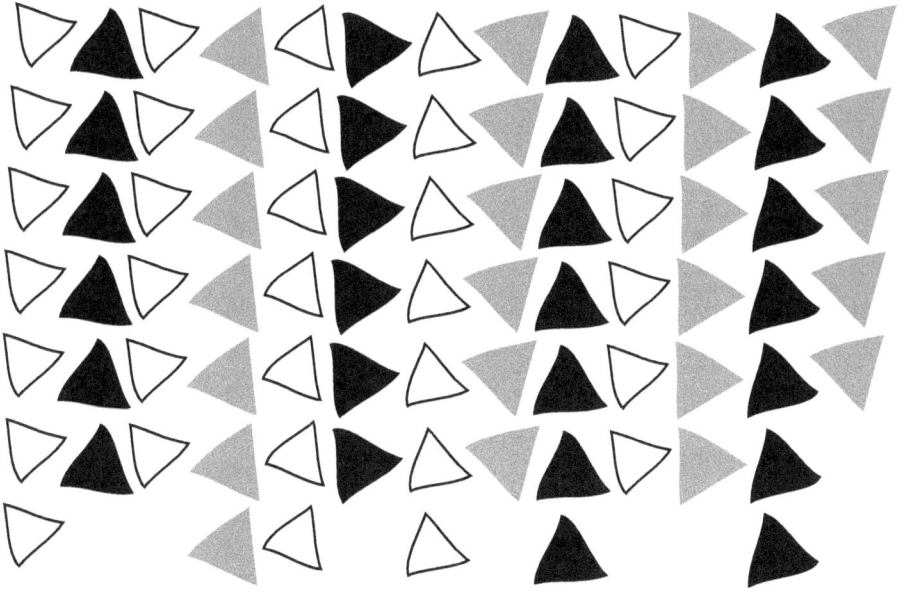

" add**verb's** *performance brought out so many wonderful emotions in me. It really reminded me why I continue to do my work with GLSEN—I do it for our youth, our future.* "

-M.S., *Tampa FL*

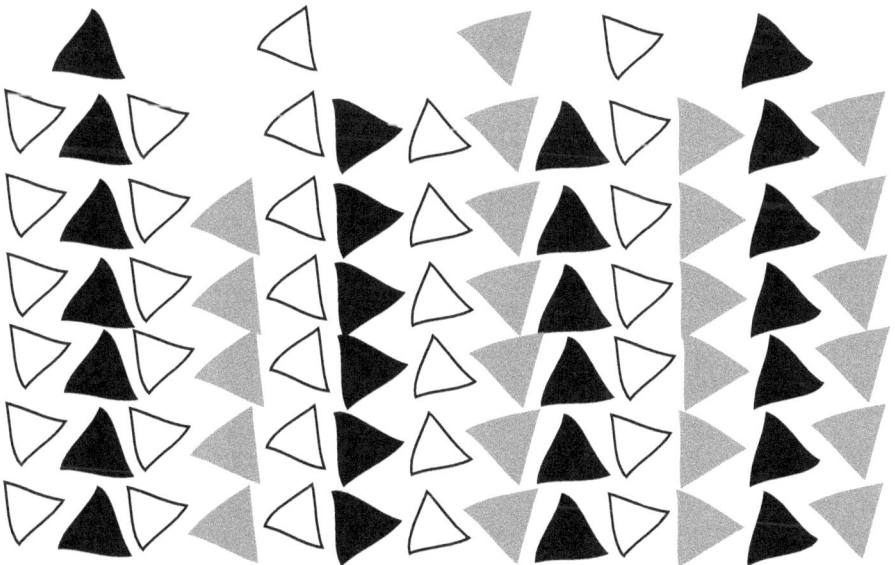

I'm Not Gay, But Thanks!
by Meredith Lamothe

CHARACTERS:
MARY-BETH, female, 9th grade.
ANIKAH, female, 9th grade.
JOEL, male, 9th grade.

(MARY-BETH and ANIKAH are sitting in a coffee shop at one table. ANIKAH gazes longingly in JOEL's direction. JOEL sits some distance from them. He is reading a book.)

MARY-BETH: Anikah? Anikah? What are you looking at?

ANIKAH: What?

MARY-BETH: You've been staring for a while…am I missing something?

ANIKAH: I have to tell you a secret. I hate to sound like I'm in middle school, but I have a huge crush on someone.

MARY-BETH: Ooooh! Who is it?!

ANIKAH: A boy.

MARY-BETH: Well yes, I kind of figured it might be a boy.

ANIKAH: Guess.

MARY-BETH: Ummm…give me a hint…is he in our class? Is he…cute? Does he hang out…in this coffee shop?

ANIKAH: Yes, yes, and yes.

MARY-BETH: Is he in here now?

ANIKAH: *(Smiles)* Yes!

MARY-BETH: Okay then it's obvious, it's the dreamy and mysterious coffee boy behind the counter!

ANIKAH: You think he's dreamy? No, it's not him.

MARY-BETH: *(Looks offstage, looks a little worried)* Mr. Jennings?

ANIKAH: Ah! Mary Beth! Of course not!

MARY-BETH: There's nobody else in here.

ANIKAH: *(Gives her an "are you kidding me?" look, sighs)* It's Joel!

MARY-BETH: *(Pauses, dumbstruck)* But…Anikah…Joel…isn't he? Isn't Joel gay?

ANIKAH: No, what? He's not! *(Catches JOEL's eye and waves, smiling at him)* Okay, I think he knows we're talking about him. I have to go. Can you get the bill?

MARY-BETH: *(Laughs)* Sure, but I still think he's gay.

ANIKAH: Ugh. Bye, Mary-Beth. *(Exits)*

(MARY-BETH starts fumbling in her purse for money, looking down. JOEL walks over. He's well dressed, attractive, and walks with confidence. MARY-BETH does not notice him.)

JOEL: Hey Mary-Beth.

MARY-BETH: *(Startled)* Oh! Hi Joel. How are you?

JOEL: I'm good, mind if I sit down? I have a question.

MARY-BETH: No, no, go right ahead, I don't have anywhere to be.

JOEL: Cool, so…how's Anikah?

MARY-BETH: She's good...

JOEL: Oh, yeah, that's good...

MARY-BETH: Can I ask you an awkward question? It's like a really really awkward question.

JOEL: *(Laughs)* Sure, go ahead.

MARY-BETH: Well...I always kinda figured...I just thought that maybe...that you were gay.

JOEL: Yeah.

MARY-BETH: Yeah? Yeah you are? Or you knew I thought that?

JOEL: Everybody thinks that.

MARY-BETH: Well are you?

JOEL: No, but actually I take it as a compliment when people think I am.

MARY-BETH: *(Giving him a questioning look)* That doesn't make sense.

JOEL: Sure it does, what do you think of when you think of straight guys?

MARY-BETH: Hmmm...messy hair...awful sense of humor...grubby clothes...and doesn't return my phone calls.

JOEL: Hah. Well, okay, that's one way of looking at it, I guess that all makes sense. Sorry he didn't return your calls...that's too bad.

MARY-BETH: Oh it's okay, uh, I wasn't thinking of anyone specific or anything...

JOEL: *(Laughs)* Now, what do you think of when you think of gay guys?

MARY-BETH: Charming, surrounded by women...great fashion sense... and a good shopping buddy.

JOEL: Hmmm would I rather be grubby with messy hair or charming and surrounded by women?

MARY-BETH: Well that's obvious.

JOEL: Exactly, gay men are typically witty, they smell good, they know how to dance…why wouldn't I want to be considered gay?

MARY-BETH: When you put it that way…it sounds like the better option.

JOEL: That's why when people think I'm gay I say thank you—and mean it.

MARY-BETH: I never thought of it like that.

JOEL: Most people don't. But it's certainly better than getting offended.

MARY-BETH: Oh, wait, I'm sorry to get you so off track. Didn't you come over here because you had a question?

JOEL: Yeah. Your friend Anikah…we're in class together…I think she's pretty cool. Do you think she'd go out with me sometime?

MARY-BETH: I think she would definitely go out with you!

JOEL: Awesome. By the way, I have a friend who thinks you're cute.

MARY-BETH: Do people sometimes think he's gay too?

JOEL: Actually, yeah, sometimes they do.

MARY-BETH: Perfect!

JOEL: Okay, I'll let him know, we can all go out sometime. *(Smiles, gets up to leave)* And thank you.

MARY-BETH: For what?

JOEL: The compliment.

MARY-BETH: *(Laughs)* Anytime!

(Lights)

" Success is blocked by concentrating on it and planning for it... Success is shy - it won't come out while you're watching. "

Tennessee Williams, *Playwright*

Personals
by Joan Lipkin and the Apple Pie ensemble, created
under the auspices of That Uppity Theatre Company

CHARACTERS:

SAM	ALEX
CHRIS	DAN
JEREMIE	DREAM

SAM: I have this thing against people saying, "straight acting." Why is putting down femme guys so macho-ly cool? I think guys should be themselves. Drop the macho bullshit. Because even girls don't like it, so why should a guy want to put up with it?

CHRIS: When you're a teenager and you're a lesbian, you're realistically only going to have one chance a year, maybe two, to date someone. This is why you should never have relationships in January. It's a bad idea, trust me.

JEREMIE: Dating as a gay man in high school has been incredibly hard. There are two out guys, and while _____* has introduced me to a lot more young gay men, the pool is quite small, if you limit yourself to out people…which I haven't always done. And let me tell you, that's not a particularly wise choice.

SAM: Single gay man, tall, skinny. Hopeless romantic. Leftist opinions. Likes reading, talking, and holding hands during walks in the park. Doesn't suffer fools gladly. Fools need not apply. Seeking shorter, sharp, out, self aware, male homophile. Must enjoy fruitful arguments, and life's simpler pleasures.

ALEX: Tall, dark eyed, Middle Eastern guy. Intellectual, introverted, loving, romantic, and serious. Looking for a nice and loving guy who can keep the conversation going. I enjoy cuddling as I watch a good movie as much as I enjoy a nice walk in the park. I am an easy person to talk to, and no matter how hard it gets, I always have a big smile on my face.

CHRIS: Christina ,14, female 5'3" Filipino**. Dark hair. Very loyal and trustworthy. I like to cuddle. Looking for a very patient girl with a sense of humor. I am very studious, semi-athletic. Play trumpet, French horn, and trombone. I guess you could say, I enjoy music.

DAN: Hi. My name is Dan! I'm 18, but don't let my age fool you. I'm quite mature for my age. I'm 5'9", 145 lbs. I have blue eyes, brown hair, facial hair, a cute smile. I'm looking for someone who's an intellectual, a conversationalist, someone who reads and has some depth to him. I want someone mature and sweet and kind, etc. More than anything, I want someone who would enjoy relaxing with me, cuddling on the couch on a rainy Saturday night, enjoying a good movie.

DREAM: I am 16 and I am a very unique person. I love to laugh and have fun. I also love to listen. You will never know what to expect when you see me because I change constantly. I love being close and sharing happy times. And I am bisexual, so girls and guys need apply. P.S. I am *not* a ho!

JEREMIE: Single, gay, Italian male seeks lover to drink coffee, enjoy poetry, and praise the feminist/anti-war/pro animal movement. Looking forward to a long talk over a soy chai latte. No Express jeans, please.

---

* Fill in a gathering place or support, i.e. Gay Straight Alliance, the Gay and Lesbian Center, etc.
** Another ethnic group could be substituted, as appropriate.

Pain
by Alex Eisenhart

Pain…utter, sincere, pain
Pain that is indescribably unbearable
Pain from fear of being who you truly are
Like hiding in a shell that gets smaller and smaller
And tighter and tighter everyday

Hiding eventually becomes unbearable
But you feel that you can't stop hiding from
Fear of being embarrassed to be who you are
Fear of showing who you are
Not knowing whether you would be happier
Or devastated letting it out
Whether it would get better or worse

Wondering if you would be accepted by those you care about
Wondering how your life would change
Wondering if your life *would* change
Never knowing until you stop hiding
Wondering if you can
Pain…utter sincere pain

STAGING SUGGESTIONS:
Casting is flexible. See notes for "Erin" *(Page 46)*.

Tranny Next Door
by Carrie-Lynne Davis
adapted by Deacon Lasagna and Ellis Matthews

ACTOR 1:
Tranny next-door, you
Sit two feet away behind a concrete wall
Those blocks, your femininity,
And that door, your masculinity;

Walk out the door, but before
Mess your hair and bind your breasts
Like steel, like the ring on your lip,
Unlipsticked—
That keeps the words a man would say,
This man would say, almond-eyed

See the world through a boy-color brown
Like the short hairs that stand
Like erections, like firm high-fives
With big hands, unpolished with woman colors,

Like pink and red, like the colors of your heart:
You cannot rid them
Or that wall between us,
Tranny next-door.

BOTH:
Straight out of the womb
You are labeled and sorted
Stuffed into an agreed upon box
Corseted into age old structures
As rigid as that checked box on your birth certificate
One of the hugest decisions in your life has been made for you
By the violences of history

ACTOR 2:

"Actually...Kristin is Toby now."

One sibling: first my sister, now my brother. On August 12, 2006, the courts deemed it official: Kristin Wittig Davis has become Tobias K. Davis. A certified catalyst, no more hiding behind acceptable labels, "sister" and "daughter," or fumbling with guilt-ridden pronouns.

I have looked up to, with awe and envy, the same freckled smile and wire-rimmed blue eyes, all eighteen years of my life. Sister or brother, the object of my admiration remains the same. His new name crowded with complications, his new exterior crammed with controversy, "unconventional" perhaps, but only because Toby does not live in the convenience of a lie, but chooses to trust the truth of who he is.

But that doesn't mean it's easy. I have to willingly set myself up for the backlash of other peoples' insecurities. I have to face the curious and critical eyes of people's reasoning, and I never know if it is I who is being assessed or the "choices" of my brother. But the difficulties I face have never mattered because I know that Toby has and will continue to face more significant and trying situations. He has to put himself on the line every day, so the least I can do is bear a few short-lived moments of discomfort.

I was ten when Toby, then Kristin, told me he had a girlfriend. I was ecstatic, finally another playmate! I was about twelve when my parents were the only ones left calling Toby "Kristin," and I was caught in the middle, torn between loyalties. And when I was fifteen I chose sides for good. I wrote a piece called "All You Need is Love," about my experience growing up with a transgendered sibling, and parents who make mistakes.

I cried the night I entered it into a contest for publication because I knew that my mother would never look at me the same way—after she read it. I had chosen Toby, not Kristin. This would be the end of sneaking around in dread of what might happen if my parents caught me uttering his name. I was afraid of disappointing them, of hurting them, but I realized that they were misguided and looking for someone to blame for the challenges of unconventionality, which coincidentally fell onto my brother, but that was the last straw.

Why would anyone want to purposefully subject themselves to people's intolerance? He did not "do this" to anyone. He is simply being true to himself because he recognizes that there can be no happiness in living a lie.

BOTH:
Your illusion of an impenetrable gender dichotomy is so damn convincing
That it has my own biology submitting
Shaping me into something alien and painful
But I am not a prisoner
No one outside of my being can dare define me

ACTOR 2:
I'm so scared, do I need scalpels to finally feel comfortable?
Do I need to cut the parts out that don't make sense so that you all can see me?
"You don't have a dick, you are what I say you are."
The accusatory gazes, the disgust,
My otherness does not fit into the category of acceptably diverse
This is TRANS in all caps,
Because with how wide this binary ravine stretches across this hateful culture
I'll need to grow wings to get across

ACTOR 1:
You first started thinking about it when you were first introduced to gender bending. You had short hair and easily mistaken for a guy. You never really thought about it at the time.

Skip nearly four months later. You're wearing baggy shorts and shirts, pinning your chest down as much as possible. You feel a rush of happiness when someone calls you "sir" or "boyish". You want to cry when they call you "miss" or "young lady." You are no lady. Not at all.

ACTOR 2:
The most memorable moments are locked away forever. When you were 13, in class. The teacher and a boy next to you were talking about moustaches. You piped up jokingly, saying "I have a moustache!", while rubbing the peach fuzz of a moustache above your top lip. The boy said "freaky", but the teacher laughed and said, "Well, you're transgendered, so it doesn't matter if you do or not!" You nearly cried from the swelling in your heart.

And another memory involving romance. Of course. A sweet young boy that you were very close friends with. It was midnight and your phone buzzed annoyingly.

"hey do u maybe want to go out sometime"

Your breath hitched in your throat. And then you took the greatest leap, calmly rejecting the sweet straight boy and replied,

"I'm really sorry. But I have to tell you something. I'm transgendered."

You waited for what felt like an hour.

"oh ok."

"I'm sorry."

"its fine"

"You don't hate me?"

"why wuld I h8 u"

You let out a sob, smiling. The first person you told.

ACTOR 1:

The topic of dating didn't come up between you two until much later. You were at a party, laughing and watching a movie with your friends. Your phone vibrated in your pocket and you pulled it out, stilling giggling at the latest joke.

"would u like to go out wit me sometime"

"you don't care that I consider myself a guy?"

"no"

You went out to see a movie a week later. Score.

He says he really likes you. You can't help but doubt that he'd like you as a guy. You hate to doubt it, but it's true. This is your first relationship since you've come to terms with yourself. And the first relationship where your partner knows.

You've been on a lot of emotional roller coasters. You got rid of all of your "girl" clothes, now stored in a huge black garbage bag. Every time you take a shower, you stare at your bare chest, hating your breasts even more with each passing day. They look awkward on your chest. You just wish they were gone.

You haven't shaved in ages. If you were still the same person you were two years back, you'd be freaking out. But you're not. You and your boyfriend sit on the couch, his arm around you and your head on his shoulder. Your gaze falls on your leg next to his. You smile at how similar they look.

ACTOR 2:
You've always wanted to be a diva. Ever since you were little. You loved the glitter and sparkles. You're in love with the glam rock era. You really want to be glamorous and fabulous, but you can't wear tight clothes without being called "miss." You want to be effeminate, but still be a guy. You want to be beautiful and an eye catcher. But right now all you can do is wait.

ACTOR 1:
You were 19 when you started taking testosterone. It was really expensive. Your parents helped a lot, but you still had two jobs to help yourself. At first, it didn't feel like all that much. Then, BAM!!! Over the time of taking it, your breasts shrank reasonably and your peach fuzz moustache actually became a moustache! Yeah, the excessive acne wasn't fun, but you felt insanely fulfilled.

ACTOR 2:
And he stayed the entire time, helping you through the constant mood swings and the growing pains. You weren't exactly manly, but you definitely felt like it.

Finally, the time arrived and you decided you were ready to rid yourself of your now small breasts. You had saved enough money along with your parents help. They were small enough that the doctor could do the drawstring procedure. Take out the remaining fat after the hormones, pull the skin down and stitch.

ACTOR 1:
When you woke up from your drug induced sleep your brother was sitting at the foot of the bed, texting. Your parents were sitting on the plastic chairs, whispering. And your boyfriend was clutching your hand while staring out the huge hospital window.
He felt you squeeze back and turned, smiling.
"Welcome to the world, babe."

BOTH:
Best wake up call EVER!

ACTOR 2:
Back at your apartment, you peeled off your shirt in front of the mirror. You've heard stories about how other post-op trans hate the scars. You love them. The faint half circles marking the end of a terrible battle. Battle scars.

ACTOR 1:
Skip three years. You have a new partner. Shortly after your top surgery, your old boyfriend split, beginning to freak out about dating a guy. Obviously he wasn't good for you in the first place.

ACTOR 2:
You met your new boyfriend at a Day of Silence celebration. A huge rally followed by an equally huge concert. The concert had everything. Music, poetry, darg, dancing. It ended at midnight.

ACTOR 1:
You were a drag performer that night, dancing and singing your heart out to glam rock songs. The crowd roared approval and you bowed low. At that time, you still hadn't had bottom surgery, so it was a little easier to dress up. None of that "tuck away" stuff.

Backstage, you ran into him. Another drag performer, how ideal! He was wearing black high heeled boots and a frilly red skirt along with a tight purple top. He had amazing eyes, one emerald green, one dark blue. He had light fluffy bright blonde hair, curving around his soft features. Astoundingly beautiful.

ACTOR 2:
He was even beautiful as himself. Tight pants and pastel v-necks and such. He actually looked at you. At you. Not quizzically like he was trying to solve a puzzle. He saw who you were. You loved that.

He was there for you for your bottom surgery. And he didn't run off afterwards. When you woke up, he was there replacing the vase of roses on your bedside table. He smiled that bright, toothy smile and kissed you gently, pushing the slightly sweaty hair from your forehead.
"I'm a real boy now."

You croaked, throat dry from lack of water.
"Yep. You really are. A real boy."
And you know what?

BOTH:
I
ALWAYS
WAS.

STAGING SUGGESTIONS:
This piece can be adapted for an ensemble, or more than two actors. Get creative—break it up into more pieces, or shorten it in a way that stays true to the complete version. This is a challenging piece. Be sure to carry the energy throughout the piece, the change in pace and intensity, use of space and pauses. Think about a sense of beginning (why is it urgent to tell this story?) and a sense of arrival at the end (what note do you want to leave the audience holding?).

" *Imagine*
being a teenager
and things are so intense,
imagine that on top of that
you are a part of
a marginalized group
that society is trying
to make invisible. "

- Out & Allied Actor

Absolving Yesterday
by Jake Johansen

As I sit here and reminisce
I'm reminded of the things I've missed
The childhood I never had
The adolescence that was never there
The rearing that so oft was bare

I hid in the shadows and behind dark walls
Concealing truths by bouncing balls
Proving false points to friends
Was my only dividend
Buying time to slink farther away

The setting of my blooming
Was the onset of my dooming
You can't be who you really are
When others take the place
Of God's own judgment
God's disgrace

So you learn to cope with slang and spit
Writing it off as though this isn't it
That life will one day be free
And gay

Indeed that day has finally come
But what price was paid through my days of glum?
What have I really become?

Am I a man of pride?
A man who no longer has to hide
In alleys and trenches and dark movie houses
From parents and siblings and husbands and spouses
Am I as I should be?

After finally breaking free from bondage
I can honestly say without much correspondence
Quite frankly,
No

A piece of me is gone
Time has past it's been so long
Since the careless days of my youth
Which indeed I have missed
Which I spent adrift

Consumed by guilt
Afraid of truth
Hiding
Waiting
But for what?
I've been waiting so long
I can't remember what for
For love?
For life?
Time ticks and tocks
While I sit by
Smashing clocks, trying to get back
What society took from me

And so the time has come my friends
To live without conviction
To laugh, to love, to see through eyes
Free from man's harsh crucifixion
To walk with my head held high
Nose to the sky
Arms out stretched
No longer a wretch
But at long last
Able to live
Able to love
To let go of my past

STAGING SUGGESTIONS:
If working this piece with your ensemble, consider incorporating unison lines as well as dividing up lines/stanzas. Perhaps one actor is central, and the ensemble supports, adds emphasis and contrast. Consider movement and stage pictures with your actors—levels, frozen images.

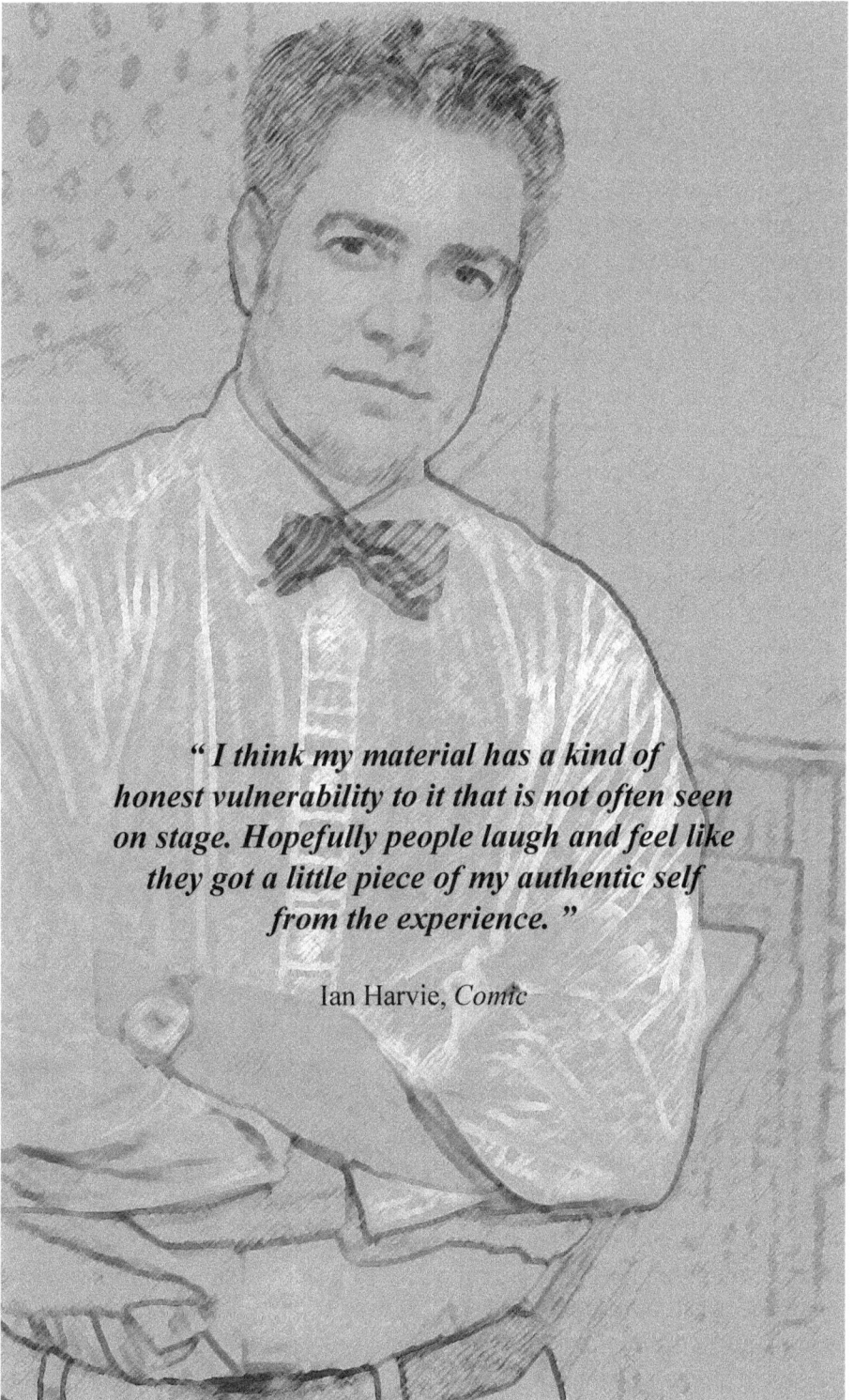

" *I think my material has a kind of honest vulnerability to it that is not often seen on stage. Hopefully people laugh and feel like they got a little piece of my authentic self from the experience.* "

Ian Harvie, *Comic*

Jeopardy
by Elyse Spike Johnson

Can we talk about pet peeves for a second? Just for one sec. Like when you tell someone something so unbelievably important to you that you are so revved up about…and then, they either say "wow" and go back to what they were doing before, or say "yeah, right. Uh-huh" and go back to what they were doing before. At least pretend to be interested. Something. Jeez. So, I guess I won't bore you guys with the story since no one else seems to care. (*Turns to leave*)

(*Turns back*) Okay, so this is what's up. After eighteen years, I finally figured out why every female stereotype made me cringe, and not just in a feminist sort of way. I liked GI Joes, I went to Boy Scout camp, ripped my dress right up the middle so it would be more like pants, and always felt awkward at sleepovers that I went to when they started talking about lip gloss and penises. Not my gig. Never really knew why until I picked up a bargain book at the library book sale. A personal memoir, written by a woman in the backwoods of Tennessee. A lesbian. I had no idea what that word meant, so I looked it up. Ahem. (*Reads from dictionary*) "A woman whose sexual orientation is to women." What? A woman who is sexually attracted to……oh boy. So, I googled it, like any normal teenager would. Bad idea. I've never cleared the history out of my computer so fast in my life. But then I did it again. And I weeded through the raunchy porn and stuff, until I found a site for older women who talked about their lives. They had coming out stories, break-up stories, marriage announcements… the whole works. I fell in love right then and there. I fell in love with women. I knew. It was the cliché lightbulb going off. I walked around for hours smiling because I felt like I had finally met myself. It was like this part of me that I hadn't known existed was suddenly there, like I could finally stop shutting the door on this one huge part of me that explained so much. It looked like, from the lingo on the website, like there were two distinct groups of lesbians: butches and femmes. It seemed like I might be a butch. Does that mean I have to like femmes? Can I wear a skirt, or does that make me a femme? I had so many questions! I had to tell someone. I realized at this point, that me running to the roof of my house and screaming at the top of my lungs "I'M A LESBIAN" may not be conducive to acceptance. I didn't know what the word was, but I knew enough to be wary about who I told. I figured that if anyone, my mom and dad would be okay with it. We had never had the sexuality talk. We never went to church or synagogue—Mom's Lutheran, Dad's Jewish—and they didn't like the word "provocative." But I'm eighteen, leaving the house for college—finally!—in a few months, and they're my parents. So, when they got home, we had dinner and did the usual routine. We then all parked it on the couch to watch Jeopardy together. During the first commercial break, I muted it. Dad asked what I was doing, and I told them I had an announcement. I steeled myself, and spat it out.

"IthinkImightbealesbiansoareyouguysokaywiththat?!" Mom and Dad exchanged perplexed glances, then looked back to me. "Try again, and slow down," Mom said. I took another deep breath, and slowed down. "I think…I think I might be a lesbian. I didn't know what the word meant until today, but it makes a lot of sense to me. Are you guys okay with that?" Again, they exchanged glances. I waited for the verdict. "We had a feeling," they said in unison, then asked me to turn the volume back up. No "that's great honey!" or even "get the hell out of our house." Just "turn the sound back on." That was it? I have this amazing, perspective altering revelation, and they want to hear what Alex Trebek has to say about Bengali culture?! I guess it could have gone worse. And then I started to think about it. Yeah, it's a big part of me. Yeah it changed my life. But if they're cool with it, then I should be too. Okay. I'm a lesbian. If it's not a big deal to them, it doesn't have to be a big deal to me. Sure, it'll be a big part of my life, but I don't have to dwell on it or go shout it to the stars. I'm a lesbian, a student, a violinist, a daughter, and a blonde. Add it to the list. What do I have for homework tonight?

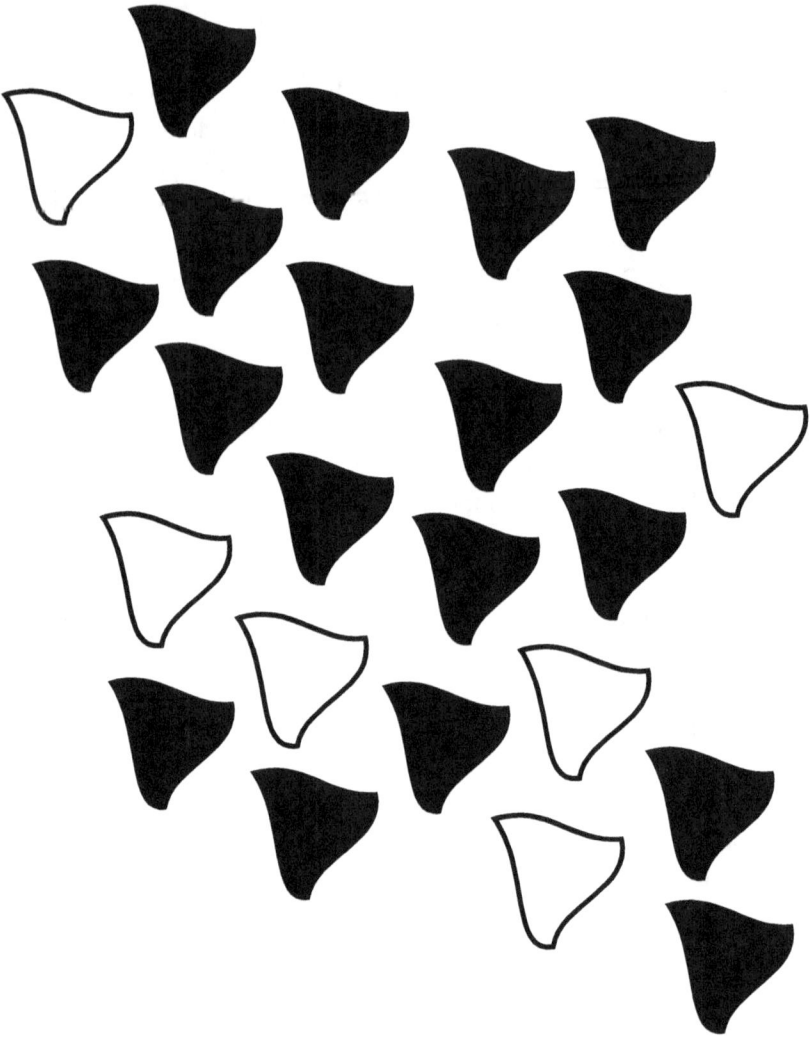

" *The work* addverb *does is powerful, evocative and unique. The messages that come out through the extraordinary performances move us all to see the power we could have in creating change.* "

-G.S., *GLSEN Northern NJ*

Sock it to Me, Baby
by Cathy Plourde

CHARACTERS:
ACTOR
SOCK

(ACTOR gets in place near the opening of the screen, waiting for a bus or the bell to ring. After a beat, the SOCK pops out, takes a look around, and then taps the ACTOR on the shoulder, maybe nibbles the ear. The ACTOR does a double take.)

ACTOR: Who are you?

SOCK: I'm yours, baby.

ACTOR: That's funny…I don't think I own any socks that call me "baby."

SOCK: I'm a special blend of cotton and "spandex-for-your-mind." If only everyone could be so lucky to have a helping hand…

ACTOR: Having an unfamiliar, *talking* sock this close to my face is not what I would call lucky. *(Wrinkling nose)* Ummmmm…that perfume is pretty powerful—

SOCK: Yes! Powerful! I have the power—the power to change the story— the power to tell you what you don't know—

ACTOR: No, I don't think so. My story is beyond the power of a talking sock. Half of everyone at school has decided I'm gay.

SOCK: I'm happy, too.

ACTOR: Not gay as in happy. Gay as in gay.

SOCK: Most people who are gay are also happy.

ACTOR: It doesn't make me happy when people call me gay.

SOCK: No, man, of course not. Those people aren't calling you gay to make you *happy*; they are doing it to make you *unhappy*.

ACTOR: I thought you were going to tell me things I didn't know.

SOCK: What you should know is that you shouldn't let other people's *hate* make you hate *yourself*. Hey, man, you are who you are, and you will be who you will be.

ACTOR: Yeah, but they hate me. I mean *hate*. Get it? *HATE*.

SOCK: I can't change them, and neither can you. But you know what, man? I gotta tell you congratulations...

ACTOR: Congratulations? I'm telling you people hate me and you're telling me congratulations?

SOCK:...congratulations *BECAUSE* you have learned how much power you have!

ACTOR: I have the power to make people hate me?

SOCK: Well, it doesn't sound so good when you put it that way, but yeah man, POWER. You have something they don't.

ACTOR: Yeah, like no friends.

SOCK: Man that hurts. You got me.

ACTOR: I'm talking to a sock who's telling me it's my friend...? I'm not so sure I need this kind of help.

SOCK: You've got friends. Real ones. Not fake friends or groupies. So you could use a few more friends, man. Who couldn't? But that's what life is about, man, making friends. It's worth looking around for good ones. And you know what, most of the friends you've got now, you won't have 10 years from now—everyone will be off finding their own groove.

ACTOR: That doesn't help me now.

SOCK: Now isn't forever, man. In a few years, you won't be in this school. You'll be living your life. Finding your own groove.

ACTOR: That assumes I make it that far.

SOCK: Hey, man, that's not funny, and not an option. You *will* be around, and you *will* have friends, and you *will* find that all this crazy stuff that seems so important...

ACTOR: Because it is...

SOCK: That feels so crazy painful...

ACTOR: Because it is...

SOCK: That seems like there is no end in sight...

ACTOR: Because there isn't...

SOCK: All this stuff will end. All this will be ancient history, man, ancient history.

ACTOR: *(Pause, while ACTOR thinks about the future and likes the sound of it)* Thanks. *(Pause)* I don't mean to be rude, but you kind of have an ancient-history aroma...

SOCK: I'm a sock, right. Not my fault. If this is how you go about making friends...

ACTOR: I've got to *HAND* it to you, you might have something there. Point well taken. I'm sorry.

SOCK: And, I've got to hand it to you, man. You know who you are. And no one can take that away from you.

ACTOR: Should we take the show on the road?

SOCK: Hey, man! You're on! We'll have a gay old time!

STAGING SUGGESTIONS:

If it's possible for there to be a screen for the puppeteer, it would allow for their script to be taped up in front of them. The other ACTOR can either have a music stand for script, or memorize. Be careful of having ACTOR just talk while looking at puppet—the audience needs to see the ACTOR's face! Also make sure the ACTOR is far enough away from the puppet to not block the view. Practice movements of the puppet in front of a mirror, so the puppet doesn't just look at the ACTOR—use up, down, sideways movements for expression. THE ACTOR can have fun with not being sure he or she wants to talk to a puppet, but since the puppet is so insistent, he or she will have no choice. This piece is better for young audiences but adults seem to get it too.

" *I think the importance of doing activist work is precisely because it allows you to give back and to consider yourself not as a single individual who may have achieved whatever but as a part of an ongoing historical movement.* "

Angela Davis, *Political Activist*

The Girl I Kiss in Bus Seats
by Marianna Bueti

There's a girl I know, a beautiful girl, named Joanie. If I could paint her face onto this page, I would, just so you could see her. She has the most gorgeous chocolate-brown eyes I've ever seen, a cute little nose, and such a pretty set of lips it could drive you mad. Her voice is sweeter than honey, as cliché as that sounds. Everything about her is just begging you to fall in love.

Though her beauty is crystal clear, her personality is the true gem worth finding. Spend a few minutes with her, and I bet she'll have you smiling so wide your face hurts. That's the true reason I fell for her, because of her brilliant personality that shines right through her. She really has the ability to light up a room.

I love Joanie and she loves me. It should be so simple, but naturally there are obstacles. There always are.

Joanie's black, I'm Italian. Any Italian out there knows how family can be a little bit racist, closed-minded. If I were to marry this girl one day, my side of the aisle would be as empty as my heart would be.

Worst of all, Joanie is a girl, and so am I.

That was our fatal mistake. If only I was a guy, everything would be right. We wouldn't have to hide how much we care for each other. It isn't fair, high school is teeming with couples who are free to show affection whenever and wherever they please. Joanie and I can barely hug without worrying who watches, who might get the crazy idea that two girls can really be in love.

It's hard to sit through religion classes, with a teacher telling me how wrong it is to love another girl. Then file out into the hallways where fag and dyke are common nicknames for those who don't fit into the preconceived mold of a regular teenager. I tell you, it makes the closet look pretty damn inviting. I'm a freak to these people, just because I wear my rainbows colored on my hands and I'm open about being a lesbian.

Yes, a lesbian. The L word. A label equivalent to social suicide in my high school. I've lost some old friends. Sometimes, it seems, those who used to shield me are now the strongest bullets. Is it worth it to be out in the open, a victim of high school feudalism, the lowest bar on the social ladder?

I look at Joanie, and my heart feels full again. Of course it's worth it. Even if I can't kiss her in the sunlight, we'll always have our secret embraces. Even though weeks passed make her tongue feel so foreign to mine, I don't mind the wait so much. One look in her eyes, and I see my world. She really is my everything.

Maybe, one day, it won't be so hard anymore. We won't have to let go, we could let our fingers lace together. We won't be confined to a bumpy bus ride to show each other the spark is still there. I love to daydream about it, wishing so hard it was true, that the future is bright and ready for us. But for now, this is how things have to be.

It's alright, as long as I have her, the girl I kiss behind vending machines, in dark movies, in the empty women's restrooms, and, of course, in our beloved bus seats.

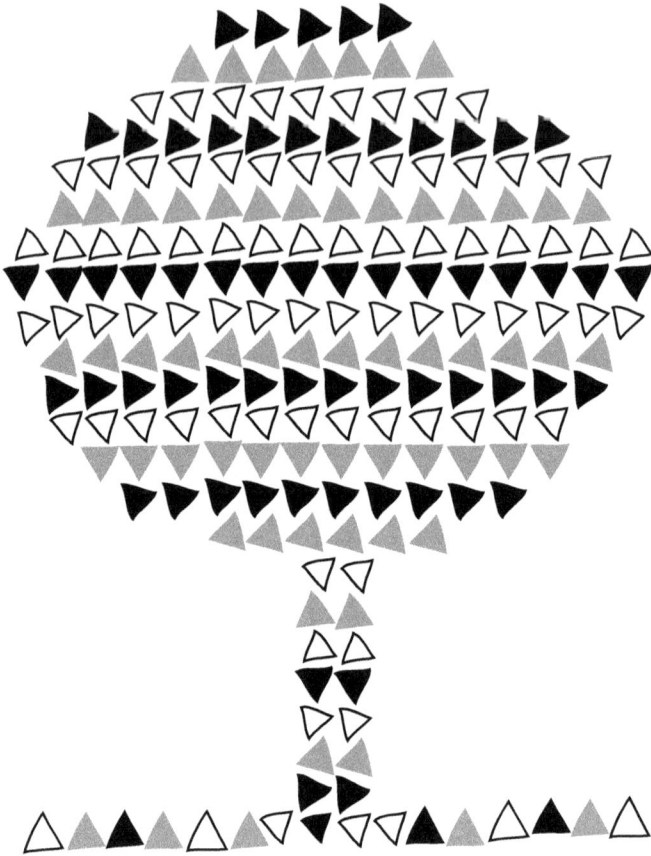

*" I have friends in my life that won't support this,
but I'm still inviting them to the show and hope
that we can talk about it afterwards. "*

- Out & Allied Actor

Liquid Gender Form
by Stephen M. Feest

As I move through the day my eyes catch males and females like separating nickels and dimes. My mind puts individuals into stupid little boxes, like mental toxins in a blink it happens before I think to ignore the dichotomy that claims so many casualties. You may not know it but a border war is blazin' and the troop levels are raisin'. It's against the suppression of androgynous gender expression. 'Cause its Barbie Abercrombie zombie wannabes, against gender benders who won't surrender to the assembly line but rather seek to redefine personality through individuality. It's perfection and perception against reflection and interconnection of liquid beings. See we're after liquid gender form, fighting against the traditional masculine and feminine norms.

It makes me ecstatic to prevent the automatic internal categorizing and create an enigmatic grey universe. I have an affinity to be something more, living at the core of my being, and not wanting to be at war with my feelings. I'm leaving behind conformity, answerability, and expectation's collapsing ceiling.

Liquid gender form: opposing folkways and mores of a culture stuck in the dark ages. We're separated between blue and pink before we're even able to blink. Individuals attempt to bust out of cultural restraints that push them back. The price paid is brutality, and even death. The statistics are overwhelming, suppressing androgynous gender expression, but our numbers are abounding.

The deaths of androgynous women and men probably don't make it into the day's headlines on CNN, though it repeatedly happens again and again. Androgynous gender expression war veterans, peaceful protesters brutalized to stop the spread. The limitations of gender expression might not be clear, but the consequences are severe. These names should be on a memorial wall rather than a body count on the headline news crawl because they, brave and tall, were in it for the long haul. Risking negative attention without apprehension.

When will we take notice of the silent killer that isn't silent but heralds his actions, only in the end claiming a panic defense to receive an infraction? Then we're left to make sense of an unfair justice system, judges on the bench, the overwhelming fumes of inequality's stench.

The latest headline murder was young gay Lawrence King, feminine and picked on for not wearing masculinity like hip-hop bling. What was this boy's crime that he died before his time? Self-actualization at the age of fifteen? His killer thought his looks, his valentine requests were too obscene. For living life in ambiguity rather than inside the boundaries of masculinity's acceptability, Lawrence King was murdered, two lives irrevocably altered, and a country left to point their finger while ignoring the fact that they helped pull the trigger.

So we're waiting on a catalyst that might not come but still we must persist in the fight to coexist. We speak our minds even though our voices shake because silence won't protect us. Oppression is the double-edged sword that cuts both ways, it cuts us when we are silent and it cuts us when we speak; either way it cuts us but its better to die for a cause then to die being meek. So we're not asking for your consideration but instead making a declaration that since the social dichotomy of our culture is killing people, now's the time to grapple, before the death tolls triple and our window of opportunity is trampled.

I'm tired of people standing on the backs of others who have wronged no one just to feel superior, when inside they are the most inferior of beings. In public they rail against the rules that they dictated, while in quiet desperation they fold into their lover's arms like weeping children, victims, even slaves to the world they've created. Empty, hollow shells of a mask that they wear, a front that conceals their true identities. But what they really hide are their inferiorities, missing complexities, and their jealousies in watching people like us live in the enigmatic grey universe of liquid gender form. Free of the complications that rigid rules present, we circumvent the boundaries living content.

STAGING SUGGESTIONS:

If you haven't seen or heard any spoken word poetry, search around on YouTube or check add**verb**'s website for an audio recording of *Tough Guys Wear Pink* (the last piece in the book). The internal and end rhyming is intentional and should be used to maximum effect—if you read it aloud looking for the rhythm of the piece you will find it almost flows all by itself, with a natural build, pace, and finish. The tradition of spoken word is bold and brave, so look your audience in the eye and be proud! Attitude is good, and look for where a smile or a soft moment can put an audience in your hand.

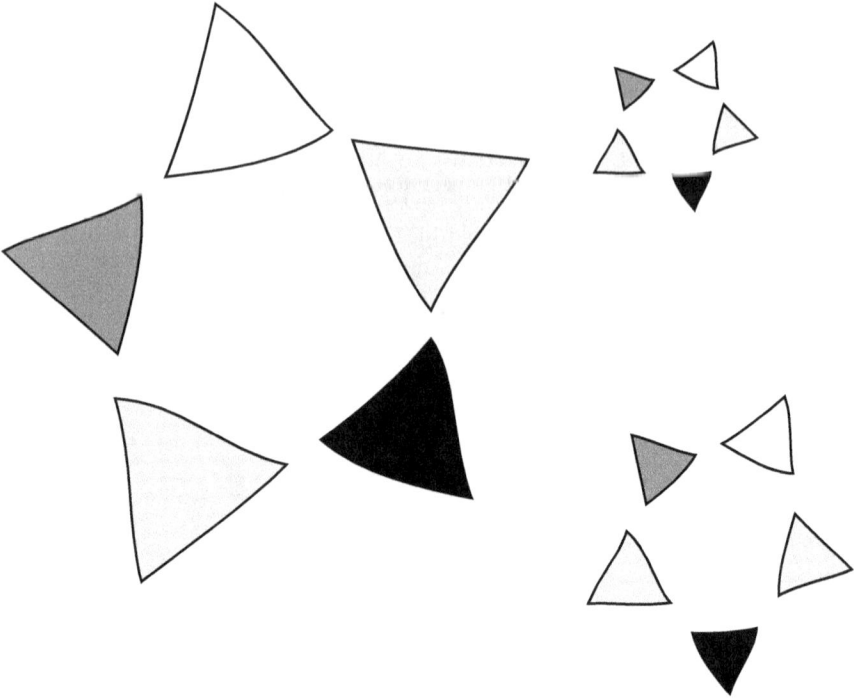

*"A brilliant performance!
I watched as a packed house rode the same wave
of emotion I was on. The level of talent and energy
was truly awe-inspiring. Thank you! Thank you!
Thank you!"*

-R. S., *Las Vegas, NV*

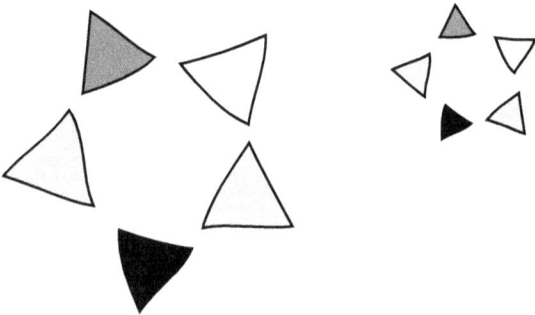

Run Away
by Brianna Suslovic

my heart pounds

um-um
um-um
um-um

why do they say those things?

"gay" and
"faggot"

rise
   and
       fall

tears
in my eyes,
blurring
everything

as I run
run away…

STAGING SUGGESTIONS:
Casting is flexible for one, three or a whole group. The premiere of this piece involved the 10-cast member ensemble. One girl stood still at center stage and began the poem. When finished, she repeated the whole piece, over and over, while one or two actors at a time entered the piece, also cycling through the piece as they moved through the space of the stage. The effect was like a song that gets sung in a round except the intensity of the words and the movement built up higher and higher, louder and louder, until with a cue from our actor center stage, everyone froze in place while she repeated the poem one more time. There wasn't a heart in the audience that didn't pound with this poem's emotion.

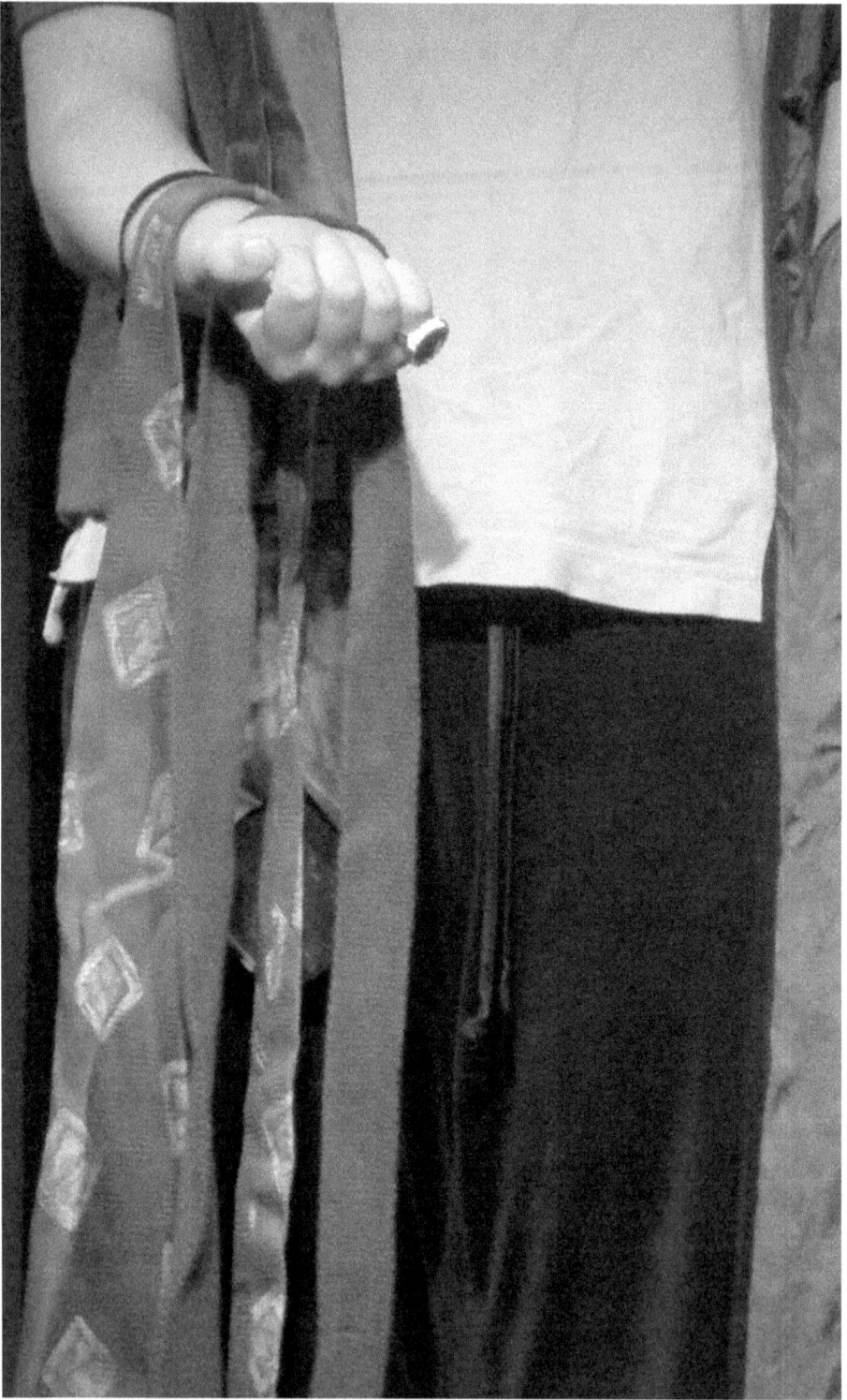

What Makes a Man?
by Micah Malenfant

I am not gay. But because I stand up for equality, people will assume I'm gay. That's just how society is these days. It just seems as if everyone's chief fear is being accused of being gay as if it were some sort of Salem Witch Trial. The difference here is that being gay isn't a bad thing and neither is supporting gay friends and family. So why are straight men so afraid of being called gay? I guess if you're considered gay then the opposite sex will give up on trying to pursue you. Yet, maybe even more importantly, if a man is called gay he feels like he is losing his manhood or risks feeling like a sissy. We then try to defend ourselves and prove that we are straight as if we are doomed if we can't. It's interesting though. All us straight guys seem to be in pursuit of showing off how masculine and straight we are, but that's not why I'm telling you I'm not gay. I'm telling you because people need to know that you don't need to be gay to support equality and supporting gay equality doesn't make anyone less of a man. A question I've often come to ponder is, "What exactly makes a man?" Stereotypes of gay men and straight men are different for most people. Straight men often think about their masculinity in terms of how they are different from women. But what about the privileges that go along with being a straight man? To be honest, I feel privileged because of things beyond my control: I'm a straight, white male. I've never been oppressed due to race, ethnicity, gender or sexual orientation. So if we have this privilege we didn't ask for, what do we do with it? I, for one, believe in fighting for equality. It's the main principle America was founded on. That's why I believe in same-sex marriage. To most that may seem weird, coming from me: the guy who declared I was straight with my very first words. Why would a straight man care about same sex marriage? I'm just standing up for my fellow men and women and what I know is right. In doing so I'm standing up for what I believe in. That's what makes a man.

The Serpent
by Megan E. Jackson

CHARACTERS:

BAYLEE, a cheerful person, but is confused throughout the whole play and frequently questions herself. When Steve asks her out she is happy, but at the same time feels some conflict between her feelings for Steve and her feelings about possibly liking girls.

SASHA, like Baylee, she's questioning herself throughout the play.

CHARLIE, raised to believe that gay people are impure and unclean. In a moment of panic he takes it upon himself to 'fix' Baylee when he finds her notebook.

PATRICK, Charlie's right hand man and looks up to him a lot. When they plan to 'fix' Baylee he is just going along with what Charlie is saying, but begins to think for himself when he sees the insanity of Charlie's actions.

STEVE, gets made fun of because he is shy and nice to girls. With the hot subject being homosexuality, Steve is being bullied about his sexuality. He's always liked Baylee and finally decides to do something about it.

SISTER MARIA CLARA, a young nun who strongly believes every word she says, but at the same time she doesn't want to seem too negative; being too negative pushes people away. She may have a perma-smile, but her underlying message is always clear.

PLAYWRIGHT'S NOTES:

Regarding the quote from the Bible: When quoting scripture nuns usually say the name of the book, chapter, and verse. Also, the line "What's up his ass?" could be changed to "What's up with him?" for younger audiences if the director finds it would be more appropriate.

(Spotlight fades in on a girl kneeling on the ground, praying. She is dressed in a typical Catholic school uniform: Plaid skirt, white button-up shirt, knee-high socks, and a tie. A large backpack sits next to her. She moves her lips silently as a classroom scene slowly lights up behind her. SISTER MARIA CLARA is lecturing a class with a ruler in hand, almost as if she is conducting.)

SISTER MARIA CLARA: God knows that those who turn against him and feel remorse will be welcomed with open arms into the kingdom of heaven if they repent. For those who turn against him are weak to temptation. For example: these liberal homosexuals, running around like they are above the word of God, fornicating, and waving their rainbow flags. But God knows that they know not what they do. They have fallen to temptation such as Eve did to the serpent in the garden. But they will realize in time that they have done wrong. They will realize in time that they are sinners.

(Lights fade on the classroom. The spotlight softens and lights come up around the girl.)

BAYLEE:…for the kingdom, the power, and the glory are yours, now and forever. Amen.

(SASHA calls from offstage.)

SASHA: Baylee! Come on! We're going to be late!

BAYLEE: Coming! *(She exits and the lights fade)*

(Lights come up on a lunchroom setting. A single long table with several chairs is placed at center stage. BAYLEE and SASHA enter, engaging in a silent conversation, and each carrying a brown paper bag. They sit.)

SASHA:…but they never even saw her leave. So I think she was in there the whole time!

BAYLEE: The whole time?

SASHA: Oh yeah.

BAYLEE: No way…

SASHA: Yeah way!

(The girls giggle.)

BAYLEE: So what do you have today?
SASHA: Ham and cheese, you?

BAYLEE: Chicken salad.

BAYLEE and SASHA: Trade?

(They switch lunches.)

SASHA: I don't know why, but it's like my mother is making lunch for you and your mother is making lunch for me.

BAYLEE: Maybe we should make our own lunch…

SASHA: Or trade mothers.

BAYLEE: Well, we're not in middle school. We are freshmen, after all.

SASHA: I know…but I do love your mom's lunches.

BAYLEE: *(She laughs and rummages in the bag)* Hey, Sash…

SASHA: Yeah?

BAYLEE: I was thinking about something Sister Maria Clara was talking about in Theology today…

SASHA: What, the gay thing?

BAYLEE: Yeah…that.

SASHA: What about it?

BAYLEE: I don't know…something…doesn't seem right about it.

SASHA: What do you mean?

BAYLEE: I just don't understand why it's so bad.

SASHA: I don't know either…I guess…maybe because they can't have kids?
BAYLEE: But there are so many people who can…why can't we just…I don't know…leave them alone?

SASHA: Well they choose to live that kind of life, don't they?

BAYLEE: People say that, but…I don't know. My uncle is gay…and I overheard my parents talking about it…they said something like, "Well it's not his fault, they can't blame him…"

SASHA: What were people blaming him for?

BAYLEE: Being gay, I guess.

SASHA: Weird…Hey did you ever think…well…about what it'd be like?

BAYLEE: What?

SASHA: Being gay.

BAYLEE: *(Laughs uncomfortably)* What…no, I…I wouldn't know… not…

SASHA: I know, I know, I know…I just mean, like…what would that be like?

BAYLEE: What? Liking girls? Uh…well I don't so…I don't know…I… this is a weird question.

SASHA: Yeah, you're right. Let's just eat before we run out of time.

BAYLEE: Yeah…let's just eat.

(Lights fade and a spot comes up on SISTER MARIA CLARA.)

SISTER MARIA CLARA: Now, nobody is saying that homosexuals are bad people, they just lost their way. If they repent and feel remorse for their evil thoughts and deeds, if they purge themselves of the life they led then they will be welcomed into the kingdom of heaven with a clean slate. Let us turn now to the story of Sodom and Gomorrah.

(The spot fades on SISTER MARIA CLARA and the lights come up on BAYLEE sitting in a chair, writing in a notebook. CHARLIE comes in and steals the notebook out of her hands.)

BAYLEE: Hey!

CHARLIE: What'cha writing in here, Baylee?

BAYLEE: Nothing! None of your business…It's homework!

CHARLIE: Homework, huh?

BAYLEE: Oh…give it back!

(PATRICK and STEVE enter.)

PATRICK: What's going on, guys?

BAYLEE: He took my notebook!

CHARLIE: Oh, come on Baylee, lighten up! *(Passes the notebook to PATRICK)*

STEVE: Maybe you should give it back, Charlie…

PATRICK: Oh, he's just having fun.

CHARLIE: Besides, what's so personal, huh? Your homework? *(Takes notebook from PATRICK)* Is it a diary?

BAYLEE: Charlie, don't! Give it back!

STEVE: Guys, just give it back…

PATRICK: Any dirty secrets in here, Baylee?

BAYLEE: Stop it!

CHARLIE: Come, on, Bay…just a peek…*(Opens the notebook)*

STEVE: Guys…

BAYLEE: NO, DON'T!

(She runs over and pushes him hard so the notebook falls out of his hands. She grabs it, looks the boys over with disgust, and exits. CHARLIE gets up.)

STEVE: *(Calling after her)* Bye, Baylee!

CHARLIE: God, what a freak…

STEVE: Serves you right, Charlie…

PATRICK: Oh, shut up Steve.

CHARLIE: Seriously, what are you a queer?

STEVE: I am not a queer!

PATRICK: I bet you are!

STEVE: I am NOT!

CHARLIE: The more you deny it...

STEVE: Shut up! In fact there's a girl I like right now.

PATRICK: Oh, really?

STEVE: Yeah, really.

CHARLIE: Who is it?

STEVE: None of your business.

CHARLIE: Is that because it's a boy?

PATRICK: I bet it is!

STEVE: Just shut up, okay! *(Starts to exit)* You guys suck. *(Exits)*

CHARLIE: God, what's up his ass?

PATRICK: Do you even need to ask?

CHARLIE: It wouldn't surprise me that Steve was one of them. God, I don't know what I'd do if he was.

PATRICK: What do you mean?

CHARLIE: Well it's not right, you know…what they do.

PATRICK: Well I don't—

CHARLIE: Hey! Are you taking his side?

PATRICK: No…

CHARLIE: Are you one of those gay rights people?

PATRICK: No! I'm just saying…nothing. I think they're weird, too.

CHARLIE: Good. 'Cause they're not right…they need to be like… cleansed or something. That's what my old man says. It's not natural and they need to be fixed.

PATRICK: Yeah…I guess so…I mean, you're right…fixed.

CHARLIE: That's right…oh crap, we're going to be late for Spanish! Come on!

(The boys exit. The lights fade.)

(Spotlight on BAYLEE at center stage. She is writing in her notebook.)

BAYLEE:…I don't understand any of this…this gay thing…it doesn't make sense. I mean…if a girl looks at another girl and thinks, "What if I kissed her…" Does that make you gay? God says that those who think these evil thoughts will be sent to fire and brimstone…I pray all the time though…I ask God for forgiveness, but I can't get this out of my head… *(Looks up)* Does this mean I'm going to hell?

(Blackout)

(Lights come up on BAYLEE and SASHA sitting at a table. CHARLIE and PATRICK enter and sit next to the girls.)

CHARLIE: Ladies.

BAYLEE: What do you want?

CHARLIE: Not friendly today, are we, Baylee?

SASHA: She told me about what you guys did.

CHARLIE: What, stole her notebook?

PATRICK: What's so wrong with that?

BAYLEE: It's my business, not yours!

SASHA: If she didn't care she'd let you see it.

CHARLIE: It's okay, I know she's got a crush on me.

BAYLEE: *(Hits his arm)* Shut up, I do not.

PATRICK: Yeah, Charlie, come on. I bet she likes me.

SASHA: You guys are stupid.

BAYLEE: Seriously.

CHARLIE: Come on, we're just having fun…unless you do like me.

BAYLEE: Gross! Not for a million dollars.

CHARLIE: Ouch, Baylee…I think you just broke my heart.
SASHA: Get lost, perv.

PATRICK: Well, well, little Miss Perfect. Do you have a crush?

SASHA: Not on your life, jerk.

BAYLEE: Come on, Sasha, let's leave these children.

SASHA: Oh, gladly.

(The girls exit. On the way out CHARLIE sneaks up behind her and grabs her notebook out of her bag.)

CHARLIE: Check it out! It's that notebook she was hiding from us.

PATRICK: But what—

CHARLIE: Look, I'm opening it whether you like it or not.

PATRICK: I don't know man…

CHARLIE: Haven't you always wanted to read a girl's diary? It's the dream, man!

PATRICK: I have always wanted to…

CHARLIE: Exactly! So what do you say, man? You with me?

PATRICK: Oh…what the hell. Let's do it!

CHARLIE: Sweet!

(Lights dim as they flip through the book. The boys pantomime reactions to what BAYLEE has written. Lights snap up and the music abruptly stop as BAYLEE runs back in the room. CHARLIE hides the notebook behind his back.)

BAYLEE: Did you guys see my notebook here? I can't find it…

CHARLIE: Notebook? Um…nope…we haven't seen it.

PATRICK: You must have left it in class or something.

BAYLEE: Oh, nobody can read that! I need it back! *(She runs offstage)*

(The boys take a moment and look at each other with wide-eyed and shocked expressions.)

CHARLIE: This isn't right.

PATRICK: I can't believe it…

CHARLIE: We have to do something about this…we have to fix her.

PATRICK: What? How? Like with holy water?

CHARLIE: No…we have to make her see that this is wrong.

PATRICK: What do you mean?

CHARLIE: By exposing her secret.

PATRICK: How are we going to do that?

CHARLIE: *(Getting angry)* Just trust me, okay!

PATRICK: Okay…

CHARLIE: Look, just do exactly what I say and it'll work. Okay?

PATRICK: I…

CHARLIE: Okay?

PATRICK: *(Hesitant)* You know…I'm always with you, dude.

CHARLIE: Good! Now come on!

(CHARLIE exits in a run and PATRICK follows. SISTER MARIA CLARA is spotlighted.)

SISTER MARIA CLARA: "Then the Lord rained brimstone and fire on Sodom and Gomorrah, from the Lord out of the heavens." Genesis 19:24

(The lights fade on SISTER MARIA CLARA and come up as SASHA and BAYLEE are walking through the hall. STEVE enters, pausing for a moment.)

STEVE: *(Calling after the girls)* Hey guys! Guys wait up!

BAYLEE: *(Cheerful)* Oh, hey, Steve!

SASHA: How's it going?

STEVE: It's okay…hey Baylee, um…I actually wanted to talk to you about something.

BAYLEE: Sure…I'll catch up with you, Sash?

SASHA: Sure. See you later, Steve.

(SASHA exits.)

STEVE: Bye, Sasha. *(Turns to BAYLEE, smiling nervously)* Hey!

BAYLEE: Hey. So…what's up?

STEVE: Um…how are you?

BAYLEE: I'm fine…what's going on, Steve?

STEVE: I, uh…okay, look um…I kind of…

BAYLEE: Spit it out.

STEVE: Okay, okay, okay…I um…I like you, Baylee.

BAYLEE: *(Not getting it)* Well, I like you, too, Steve.

STEVE: Great…well that's not…*(Sighs)* I mean I like you like you.

BAYLEE: You do…I mean…wow! You do!

STEVE: Yeah…and I was wondering…if, well…you'd like to…go out with me sometime? Like for pizza or a movie or something? My older brother is home from college so he can drive us! I mean…he has his own car and everything…

BAYLEE: I…wow…

STEVE: It's okay if you don't want to…I just thought I'd ask. Just forget it…

BAYLEE: No! Steve, I'd love to.

STEVE: That's okay, I...wait, really?

BAYLEE: Sure. But I have a better idea: how about the dance? It's tonight and I mean...well I don't have a date…do you?

STEVE: Yeah! I mean no! I mean…um…That sounds great, Baylee. How about I come by your house at about six?

BAYLEE: Sounds good. I can't wait.

STEVE: Okay, well…bye!

BAYLEE: Bye!

(STEVE exits. BAYLEE remains onstage looking positively giddy. SASHA reenters.)

SASHA: So? What did he want? What did he say?

BAYLEE: He…asked me on a date.

SASHA: Oh. My. GOD. Dish! You have to tell me everything! How did he look? How did he ask you? Was he nervous? Were you nervous? Details, woman, details!

BAYLEE: Okay, okay! I'll tell you on the way home.

(*The girls giggle and continue chattering as they exit. Lights dim. CHARLIE and PATRICK enter. CHARLIE has an armful of papers that he thrusts into PATRICK's hands. He begins looking for a place to hide. PATRICK doesn't move.*)

PATRICK: Hey, Charlie, I don't know about this…what are we even doing?

CHARLIE: Will you shut up, already? Help me look for a good hiding spot.

PATRICK: It's just…do we know that this is a real thing?

CHARLIE: It was in her diary, man! Girls never lie in their diaries.

PATRICK: Dude, it just…seems a bit…mean…reading her diary like that. And seriously, what are we going to do with all these papers? We aren't really spreading this around, are we?

CHARLIE: What, are you going to pansy out on me?

PATRICK: I'm no pansy…Baylee just seems like a nice girl and—

CHARLIE: Well, she's obviously not.

PATRICK: I guess not…

CHARLIE: Are you doing this with me or not?

PATRICK: I…fine, man…but—

CHARLIE: Just follow my lead…oh, crap! Here she comes!

(*CHARLIE and PATRICK hide as BAYLEE and SASHA enter.*)

SASHA: Pizza? Really? Wow, that's kind of…old fashioned, isn't it? I mean this isn't the 50s…

BAYLEE: Oh, come on, Sasha, it was sweet. It was old fashioned, though. We're going to the dance instead.

SASHA: Aw great!

BAYLEE: Yeah! He was all nervous and he—

(CHARLIE and PATRICK jump out from their hiding spot.)

CHARLIE: *(Menacing)* Evening, ladies.

SASHA: What do you want, you creep?!

BAYLEE: Why did you scare us like that?!

CHARLIE: We need to talk.

PATRICK: *(Still nervous)* So…where are you two off to?

SASHA: We were just walking home.

CHARLIE: Oh, yeah?

BAYLEE: Yeah. Now get out of my way, Charlie.

CHARLIE: Why should I?

BAYLEE: Look, I don't have time for another one of your games.

CHARLIE: Got somewhere you need to be?

BAYLEE: Yes! I have a date for the dance, and I'm going to be late if you don't let me by!

CHARLIE: A date, huh? Who's it with?

BAYLEE: I'm not telling you.

PATRICK: Charlie…

CHARLIE: Why? Because it's with a girl? *(He pushes her down. She hits the ground and starts to cry)*

PATRICK: Charlie, what are you doing?! *(Drops the papers)*

SASHA: Oh my god!

PATRICK: You just hit a girl!

CHARLIE: So what? She deserved it.

SASHA: Why?!

CHARLIE: She is disgusting. She writes about liking girls in her diary—

SASHA: What?

BAYLEE: I knew you took it!

CHARLIE: You weren't expecting anyone to read that, were you? Well now everyone's going to get a chance to see how gross you are. *(He grabs the papers off the ground)* See these? 500 copies of that entry in your diary for the whole school to read.

BAYLEE: *(Sobbing)* You can't!

CHARLIE: Yes I can and I will.

BAYLEE: I…was…just so confused. Please don't do this—

CHARLIE: Monday morning everyone will know who you really are and I'll be a hero for exposing you. I'll be—

(He is cut off when SASHA runs behind him and pushes him to the ground.)

PATRICK: Oh my god!

CHARLIE: Ow! What the hell?!

SASHA: *(To CHARLIE)* Next time you think that you can purge someone of their sins look in the mirror you creep! *(PATRICK looks horror stricken, Sasha turns to him)* What are you looking at? You helped him!

PATRICK: I…I…I'm sorry I…I shouldn't have….

SASHA: No you shouldn't have. You need better friends.

PATRICK: I…I do…I'm so sorry!

(PATRICK runs offstage. CHARLIE stands up, whimpering slightly and starts to exit.)

SASHA: Not such a man now, are you, crybaby?

CHARLIE: Shut up! You're both freaks! There's n-n-no place for freaks in heaven!

BAYLEE: *(Standing)* Go to hell!

(He exits.)

SASHA: Are you okay?

BAYLEE: *(Gives her a tight hug)* I don't know what I would have done if you hadn't been with me.

SASHA: You're my best friend, do you really think I would have let that jerk hurt you?

BAYLEE: You must be my guardian angel.

(They begin to pull out of the embrace as STEVE enters holding a flower. BAYLEE and SASHA look at each other for a long moment then kiss; this is the moment they've been so curious about. STEVE sees this and gasps. They quickly turn to see him.)

BAYLEE: Steve! *(STEVE says nothing, but throws the flower on the ground and exits)* Steve, wait! Hold on!

SASHA: Um...I...I have to go.

BAYLEE: Wait...no I...this is so confusing...I can't...

SASHA: Baylee, I...I have to go home...

BAYLEE: Sasha, wait!

SASHA: Baylee...

BAYLEE: Sasha, please don't stop talking to me...you're my best friend.

SASHA: Bay, I'm not going to stop talking to you...just...call me when you get home, okay?

BAYLEE: But—

SASHA: *(Smiling)* I'm going to get yelled at if I don't get home soon... Trust me. everything is going to be okay. *(Starts to exit, but pauses)* You think this is what it's like?

BAYLEE: You mean...being, well, you know.

SASHA: Yeah...'Cause if it is I...*(Kisses her on the cheek)*...well...I'll talk to you later.

(SASHA runs off and BAYLEE is left onstage. BAYLEE is spotlighted.)

BAYLEE: *(Happily)* Talk to you later.

STAGING SUGGESTIONS:

A director can set aside all lighting and set suggestions and perform the piece in a minimalistic fashion. All actors could remain onstage at all times: BAYLEE and SASHA standing stage right, SISTER MARIA CLARA sitting on a stool upstage center, and CHARLIE, PATRICK, and STEVE standing stage left. The actors can turn their backs and face the wings when the script indicates that they exit the stage. This piece has been performed with as little as one stool, BAYLEE's backpack, a notebook, a pen, and a stack of papers (photocopies from BAYLEE's notebook). If actors are not costumed, SISTER MARIA CLARA could hold a rosary or wear a cross to indicate that she is a nun.

Linda
by Joan Lipkin

CHARACTERS:
TOMMY, five to six years of age.
BETHY, age four.

SETTING:
A sandbox of a playground.

NOTE:
Two children in a park. They can be played by teenagers or adults.

TOMMY: My daddy's going to buy me a horse. He's going to buy me two horses and a Nintendo. He flies for United Airlines and gets to fly all over the world. What's *your* daddy do?

BETHY: I don't know. I don't have a daddy.

TOMMY: Everybody has a daddy.

BETHY: Not me.

TOMMY: You mean he went away.

BETHY: No. I don't have a daddy.

TOMMY: Then he must be here. Everybody has a daddy. If you don't have a daddy, how'd you get here?

BETHY: Love. My mommy said before I was born that she didn't want them to take me away like they did Linda's little girl so she made me with love.

TOMMY: That's the dumbest thing I ever heard. Everybody knows that the daddy puts his pee-pee in the lady's…you know…and a baby grows in her stomach. I know what you are. It's a bad word. You're a bastard.

BETHY: I am not.

TOMMY: Are so.

BETHY: Am not.

TOMMY: So.

BETHY: I don't care. I have a Linda.

TOMMY: A Linda? What's that?

BETHY: Like a daddy, I guess, only she's a lady.

TOMMY: You mean your mommy. Your mommy's name is Linda.

BETHY: No, my mommy's name is…Mommy. Linda's like my other mommy.

TOMMY: Wow. Two mommys. Do they tell you what to do all the time?

BETHY: Sometimes. Mostly my mommy does. Linda's real nice. She reads me stories and taught me how to tell time. Sometimes, she buys me chocolate chip cookies at the Galleria when my mommy's not looking. She loves us a whole lot. We're going to the zoo tomorrow.

TOMMY: I love the zoo. Are you going to the Planet of the Apes?

BETHY: Yeah. It's my favorite.

TOMMY: Me, too. I'm sorry that I called you that bad word.

BETHY: It's okay. Linda says it doesn't matter what people call us. Sticks and stones may break my bones…

TOMMY: But names will never hurt me. *(Shyly)* My name is Tommy.

BETHY: My name is Bethy.

TOMMY: Hi.

BETHY: Hi. *(Now they're friends)* Do you want to go with us to the zoo tomorrow? You can bring your daddy.

TOMMY: I don't know.

BETHY: We go a lot. Linda likes to ride the train and drink frozen Cokes. Don't you want to go? It'll be fun. We can all go together. Maybe your daddy can ride us in his airplane. I've never been in an airplane before.

TOMMY: I don't know. My daddy doesn't live with us. He lives in Chicago.

BETHY: Oh.

TOMMY: He calls me sometimes. He makes piles of money. He's going to buy me a horse. My mom said he should send us some money on time instead of galla, um…galla…gall-a-vanting around the country.

BETHY: Oh.

TOMMY: Yeah. She doesn't like him anymore. But I do. *(Crying softly)*

BETHY: *(Comforting him)* Yeah. Well, that's okay. You could still go with us to the zoo. We can go to the Planet of the Apes. I'll ask Linda. She always says I can bring my friends. Sometimes she brings her friends and then we all ride the train.

TOMMY: I wish I had a Linda.

" *For a very long time everybody refuses and then almost without a pause almost everybody accepts.* "

Gertrude Stein, *Author*

Once Again
by Elyse Spike Johnson

Three? Four? No, five. It's the fifth time in a week. Not bad, considering the past trend. I feel the dials pressing into my back as I struggle around the hand. Feeling as though the cyclic numbers are branding into my skin, I stifle my gag as eau de gym sock wraps around my nostrils. It's my own fault, I suppose. I was stupid enough to admit it to one untrustworthy person, and now it's day five and it's me vs. them again. I think there are four of them but my vision is starting to go as my brain starts to lose oxygen to the rest of my body. I feel the hand start to release and I crumple to the floor. I try not to take it personally. After all, they are the soccer team and I am the new school fag. Did I have it coming? Does the fact that I would rather share my bed with another man make me a bad person? With everything I've heard over the years, it seems that the vast majority of the population would seem to think so. Sodomite, queen, fag, pansy, queer, faerie, pussy. Strings of words that blend together as I hear them over and over again, whispered in my ear as I walk to class, thrown at me as I walk to my car, screamed across the lunchroom, and carved into my locker. Words. Each of them has a story, a meaning, an origin. Who was the first homosexual to be called a fag? What I would give to hear their story, the story of all of those before me that have been oppressed. And never mind just the gays, or just the African Americans, or women, or any particular group that has been thrown under the bus time and time again by society at large. But back to me. I finally start to see the locker room again. It's funny that the only time I really see it is from the floor. I never seem to last long vertically under my own power in here. As I finally get onto my knees, Mr. Brady comes in and yells at me to get off my lazy pansy ass. Does he know? Or is it just another word to him too?

Natural Stance
by Victoria Baker

We resume our natural stance,
One hand on your hip,
One hand on my thigh,
May there be a string to connect our estranged,
Beating Hearts.
Friction equates to warmth,
I need this warmth,
Beneath the intensity,
Of your eyes,
A stirring of wanting,
For I want the same.

We resume our natural stance,
Your hands on my face,
Taking in the warmth of steam,
From air-chilled breath,
You remark about the smell of coffee,
I must agree.
My fingers are freezing,
Your hair still wet,
From the shower we took,
Liquid heat,
Down the curves of your body.

The thump of my boots,
The crunch of dead leaves.
Your frizzled orange hair,
The freezing kisses of the air.
I smell it,
The burning of logs,
The smoke that rises into the unreal gray sky,
I remark about heaven,
You smile and reply,
If it exists.
Your lips against mine,
The taste of cream,
Of the pastry we shared.

I need your warmth.

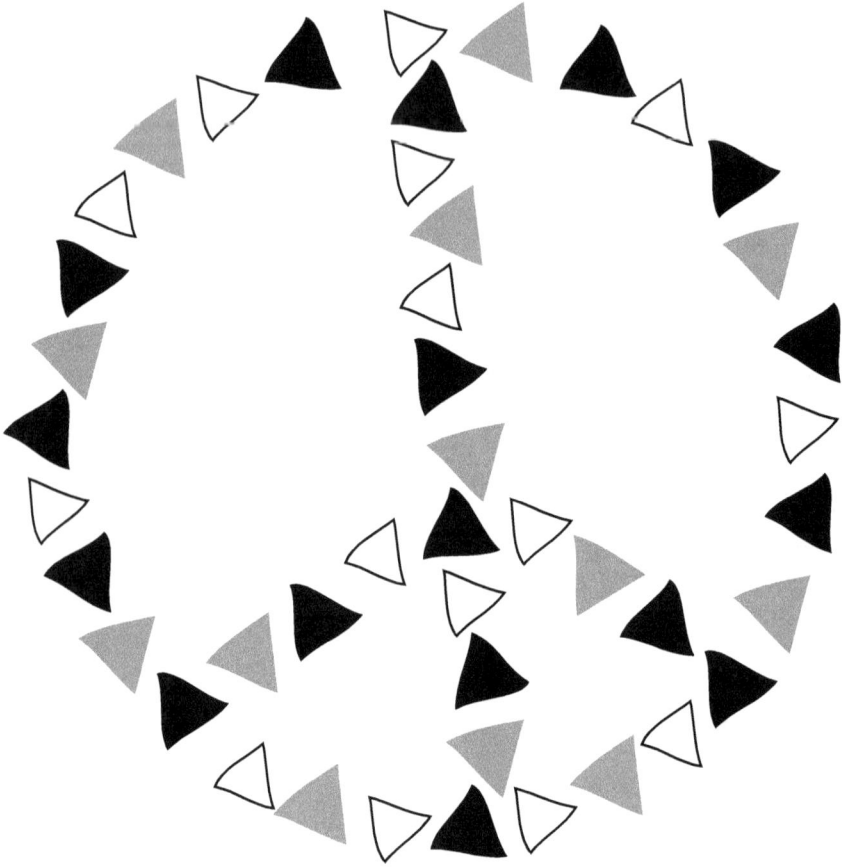

" You folks are so amazing—I was incredibly impressed.
Thank you so much for sharing with us. "

-T.G., *Washington, DC, Anchorage, AK*

Tea With Dad
by Cathy Plourde

CHARACTERS:
GEORGE, a man.
JARED, a man.
DAVE, a boy.
OFFICER BUTTINSKY, female to male, in transition.

SETTING: A living room.

GEORGE: *(Composes self, calls offstage)* David? Son, we need to talk.

DAVE: *(Offstage)* Sure daddy, I'm almost finished with this macramé plant hanger just let me tie this one off.

(DAVE enters. DAVE is a bit over the top flamboyant, employing stereotypically gay gestures and tone.)

DAVE: So, pops, what's on your mind?

GEORGE: We need to talk man to man here.

DAVE: Fierce. You're scaring me.

GEORGE: There are some things we need to have out in the open.

DAVE: Daddy, I've been very open with you, and you just don't want to hear it.

GEORGE: I've talked to your mother…

DAVE: I thought this was a man to man talk…

GEORGE: And if you want to talk to someone, a professional, about what you're going through…

DAVE: You want me to see a shrink? I'm gay, dad, not confused.

GEORGE:…we'd be happy to pay for it.

DAVE: Okay, now this has taken a turn for the surreal…can we start this conversation over?

GEORGE: This charade has gone on long enough, Dave.

DAVE: I'm sure I don't know what you mean.

GEORGE: I mean I know you're not gay.

DAVE: I am gay.

GEORGE: No, you're not.

DAVE: Daddy, I am. I am I am I am.

GEORGE: No, David. I am gay. Jared is gay. I know gay. You are not gay.

DAVE: How can you talk to me this way?

GEORGE: Come on. It's embarrassing. All of our friends know that you aren't gay, and it's very difficult to explain why you're pretending to be gay.

DAVE: This is so homophobic I can't stand it.

GEORGE: I'm not homophobic.

DAVE: I wonder how many thousands of other gay boys and girls in this world have parents who accuse them of faking being gay?

GEORGE: If you were gay, I'd be very happy for you. I'd love and accept you. Just as I accept you now.

DAVE: You don't accept I'm gay.

GEORGE: Jared??

JARED: *(Offstage)* Davie, honey I love you and you most certainly are not gay.

DAVE: But you won't accept me because you don't believe me? I do macramé, I bake, I study fashion…

GEORGE: That doesn't make you gay, David. Lots of people do those things and it has nothing to do with sexuality, nothing to do with orientation. This is life, real life, and you need to stop pretending it's some Hollywood movie script.

DAVE: Oh this isn't Hollywood, Daddy. This is second string indie, fringe festival digital.

(JARED enters with a tray with tea and cookies.)

JARED: I don't mean to interrupt—I just thought you all might like some tea and cookies. I've got a pot of Celestial Seasonings Herbal Tension Tamer all ready. Lots of B-vitamins to make everybody feel happy. Help yourself to the goodies—Dave, your favorite, lemon squares.

DAVE: I can't eat right now.

GEORGE: I know it was difficult for you when your mother and I decided to split up. *(No response from DAVE)* And I have always been proud of how you understood and accepted that I wanted to spend my life with Jared, and that your mother, on the other hand—

(Interrupted by a knock.)

BUTTINSKY: *(Offstage, female presenting as male)* Open up—I'll have to take this door by force if someone doesn't open up right now.

DAVE: I'm trying to open up. You won't let me.

GEORGE: *(Opening door)* Just a minute, Officer—can I help you?

BUTTINSKY: I'm from the Department of Homoland Security. We've had a report that there has been some recruiting of a minor going on here.

GEORGE: I beg your pardon? Homoland? Security? Minor?

BUTTINSKY: Two gay males living here?

GEORGE: Yes, and our son…

BUTTINSKY: I'll have to ask you to step aside.

JARED: Warrant! Warrant!

GEORGE: Right, dear—Officer, I'll ask you to identify yourself and present your warrant.

BUTTINSKY: I'm Officer Buttinsky, and as this is a question of Homoland Security, under the Protect Us From All We Fear Act, I don't need to show you...

GEORGE: I don't know this Department of Homoland Security...can you explain?

DAVE: Do you have to be gay to work for Homoland Security? I may need to be supporting my self soon, and could use a job.

JARED: Oh—I heard about these people—they come in and take people away to Bay of Gay Island, and for months and months no one even gets to...

BUTTINSKY: Everyone—enough—quiet! One at a time! First—the Department of Homoland Security was formed shortly after the attack on our patriarchy's family jewels—I mean our family *values*, which has resulted in threatening the existence of the American nuclear family.

Second, to answer your question young man, no, no gays are accepted into the Department—though we did try Don't Ask Don't Tell for a period in the 90's.

Third—there is no Bay of Gay Island—that is suburban legend.

And I do not need a warrant, as I was saying, thanks to the Protect Us From All We Fear Act. I'm here on suspicion that because you are two gay males, you are trying to recruit a minor to your way of life.

DAVE: If only, Officer Butinsky—I keep trying to tell my Dads that I am gay...

GEORGE and JARED: He's not gay.

DAVE: AND, YES, EXACTLY. They keep telling me I'm not gay.

BUTTINSKY: Well, if you are living with two gay men, they must be trying to sexually molest you, are you alright? Have they ever touched your genitals?

DAVE: Does changing my diapers count?

BUTTINSKY: When did you last wear diapers?

DAVE: I don't know…

JARED: He toilet trained at 2 years and two months.

BUTTINSKY: So, are you telling me that there's been *no* unwanted touching of your person?

DAVE: There was the time Dad grabbed my arm to get me to leave the Gap when I wasn't ready.

BUTTINSKY: I'm afraid that doesn't count, son. You have to give me something to work with here if you want me to protect you.

DAVE: I'm not sure I need protecting from my parents…

BUTTINSKY: Well, we can't have gay people trying to recruit minors...

DAVE: You don't understand—they won't let me be gay.

BUTTINSKY: Oh really? Well, that's admirable of them, even if they are gay themselves.

DAVE: What are you talking about? You say it like it's a terrible thing. Don't you get it either? I want to be gay. I really really want to be gay.

BUTTINSKY: *(Visibly more and more uncomfortable)* Son, this sounds like some sort of advanced brainwashing reverse psychology technique—I think I'd best take you into protective custody...

DAVE: Shut up, would you?! Look at them. Look at how happy they are. They have each other. They enjoy their lives. They are the greatest, most well-adjusted people I know.

BUTTINSKY: David…

GEORGE: David, it's okay…

JARED: You are the nicest kid ever.

DAVE: I want what they have. I want to have real love in my life. I want to have a family someday.

GEORGE: Is that what this is about? You are afraid you won't find love in your life?

DAVE: All the heterosexuals I know end up divorced. I don't want that. I want to be happy.

GEORGE: You can be happy. You can be gay, you can be straight, you can be happy. You can experiment all you want, and that's okay. But Dave, you really are not gay.

DAVE: You don't know. You aren't me. You can't tell by looking. Maybe you think you know. Maybe you're right. But it's for me to find out.

GEORGE: *(Finally, he gets it)* Dave. You're right. It's your life. Only you really know yourself best.

JARED: *(Last ditch effort)* Davie. Look here at this nice heterosexual police officer. Officer Buttinsky, you are heterosexual yes? *(BUTTINSKY hesitates, panics, nods)* See? Look how happy the police officer is—he's a bit misguided in his job, of course, because we don't need a Protect Us From All We Fear Act—but he's happy, look at him...

BUTTINSKY: I'm not happy.

JARED: See? David, this police officer—wait—what?

BUTTINSKY: I'm not happy. In fact, I'm not a man, I'm a woman. But I want to be a man.

JARED: Ooooh! Pre-op?

BUTTINSKY: I'm trying to save up enough money for hormones and then maybe an operation—but I don't know yet. I didn't think anyone would find me out working for Homoland Security. BUT it's all a sham. I'm not protecting anyone from anybody. There wouldn't even be a Department of Homoland Security, except for this Protect Us From All We Fear Act...

DAVE: Sounds like we do need Homoland Security—to make sure it's safe for anyone who wants to be gay to be gay.

BUTTINSKY: But I'm not gay, see, I'm actually bi.

JARED: Ahhh! The whole gender versus orientation issue. Of course. It can be quite complicated.

BUTTINSKY: I have a younger brother who's gay, however. Our parents haven't quite known what to make of us.

GEORGE: I think I can sympathize with your parents, Officer.

JARED: Officer Butinsky, will you stay for tea? I'd love to hear about your hormone treatment plans...Will your insurance plan cover it? And how old is your little brother and is he dating anyone?

DAVE: So Pops...

GEORGE: If you say you're gay, Davie, then, yes, okay, fine—I believe you.

DAVE: Well, I was just going to say that I can see you're just trying to be a good dad, protecting me and all.

JARED: That's my Georgie—protecting us all.

BUTTINSKY: *(Eating another cookie, getting cozy)* Can I have the recipe?

(Lights)

Tough Guys Wear Pink
by Stephen M. Feest

If tough guys wear pink does it matter what the other guys think?
Maybe it isn't whether they wear pink but that they wear it tough.
Emotions, fears, pain; a man is tough when he hides all that stuff.
Walkin' around with that gansta swagger, lookin' at someone like me,
in the eyes of traditional masculinity. Your smirk and your words don't
faze me, 'cause when it comes to your opinion, I agree. If tough guys
wear pink then I wear blue. Wearing a mask that hides who I am inside
isn't something I aspire to. In your segment of the population I'm the
in-your-face truth. Standing here taking your insults like bullets, I'm a
queer youth.

If tough guys wear pink does that mean that they reject the cliché that
guys who wear pink are usually gay? What if you're not only gay but
genderqueer, androgynous and have gender flexibility? Maybe you hold
hostility out of jealousy for my ability to express versatility in liquid
gender form. I have the ability to transform norms and reform conformity.
But every time I learn that there are still people out there like Sally Kern,
who've crossed the point of no return, it's like a cigarette burn to my
pride. To be spurned and cast aside, denied my humanity under so-called
Christianity. And without concern they cast their eyes from my friends
who continue to commit suicide. I see you gaze upon me, head-to-toe
scan. A smirk on your face, somehow you find distaste in who I am.

If tough guys wear pink do they stop and think why someone like me is
such a threat to their masculinity? Tough guys are usually the gay bashers,
dripping our blood on the cold concrete when inside their thoughts and
emotions leave them incomplete. Why must I be beaten in the back
streets, where every walk home is trick or treat? What is it that makes
you a man? Is it part of God's plan? For the Bible tells me so, is that how
you know? To decide who is a friend or a foe? Maybe I'm your bro or
just some John Doe. But why must I be discreet and defeated, retreat and
deleted from this world? To be a piece of trash for the trash can, simply
for being who I am: a gay man.

It just so happens God and I have been tight since birth; he's continued to help me through hell on earth. I've been on the operating table so many times, that God has had his chance but he declined. So I must be on his good side, allowed a little pride, to know inside that he's my guide and there isn't any man who's gonna tell me how to live right. 'Cause God and I are tight.

If tough guys wear pink, then they should stop and think that one day they would have been brutalized, for representing something slightly feminine risking being cast aside, for breaking the limits of traditional masculinity, and being free to express themselves individually.

If tough guys wear pink then they should realize the evolution of progress and honor those who are brave enough to address the limits of sexuality and gender in the face of protest. And be impressed with the finesse that people like me possess when faced with hate for choosing to follow what happens to be innate.

 Audio version online at
www.addverbproductions.org

" It is the duty of youth
to bring fresh new powers
to bear on social progress.
Each generation of young people
should be to the world
like a vast reserve force
to a tired army.
They should live
the world forward.
That is what they are for. "

Charlotte Perkins Gilman, *Author*

add**verb's**
OUT & ALLIED HANDBOOK
A guide to producing performances

You've read the anthology. Now what?
There are lots of options…

> Keep it on your shelf, and re-read upon occasion.

> Re-think and improve how you are an ally to others.

> Share the book with your friends, a teacher or group leader.

Or, take your involvement a step further…

> Write your own piece.

Or, succumb to our ulterior motive and master plan…

> Put on a show.

If you decide to put on a show, why do it half-way? Why not figure out how to put on a show in a way that will not only show off any local brilliant acting or playwriting talent, but will make your community safer, stronger, happier?

And since you decided to put on a show, how about sharing with add**verb** what you've done? We want material for the website and for the next volume of Out & Allied:

- Video links to performances of your work
- MP3 recordings of your versions
- Remarks, advice, and feedback to share with others how things went in your production
- Success stories of what happened because of your show
- Personal insights to how the show changed you, or how you think about the world
- And of course—submissions of new works you've developed, with release forms if you wish us to put them on our website or in the next anthology (if we don't have a release, we can't use it!)

In this next part of the book, you will find add**verb's** production kit and activist information. It's a guide to making the kind of theater that encourages dialogue and action, not just after the show, but in the weeks and months and years after *that*.

We've included ideas on everything from getting a cast together, to rehearsal scheduling, to setting up for a positive talk-back experience. In addition to sample organizing tools, you'll find helpful information such as:

- An interview with an award winning GSA activist
- Glossary of LGBTQ terms
- A Student Bill of Rights
- Identity Spectrums Pinwheel
- An index of LGBTQ theatre projects in the US
- Tips on writing for the stage
- Words from other activists and artists

Take what's useful and leave the rest.

Oh, and break a leg!

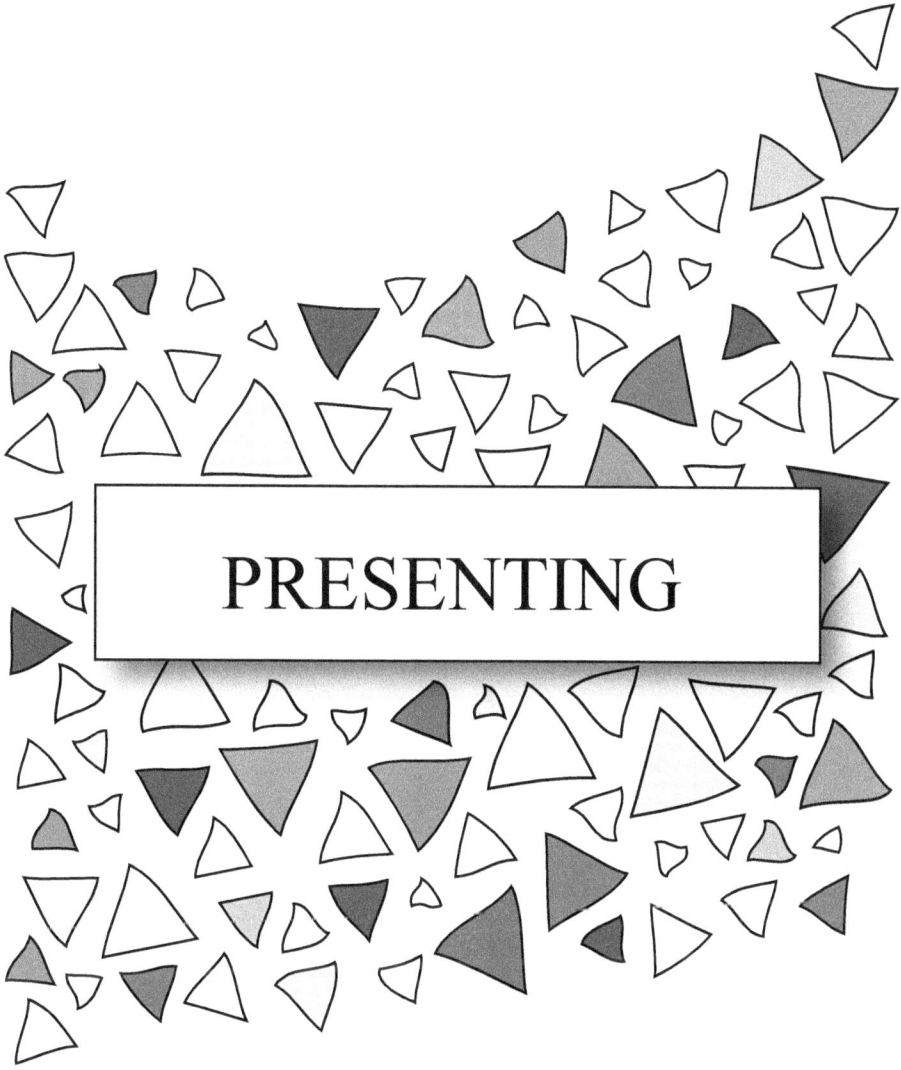

PRESENTING

OUT & ALLIED IN YOUR COMMUNITY

WHY, WHEN, FOR WHOM?

These performance pieces can be used for…

Training for Civil Rights Teams,
Gay-Straight Alliances (GSAs) or other student leadership groups,
National Coming Out Day (October 11th),
Way to end the National Day of Silence,
Diversity Week,
LGBTQ Health Awareness Week,
Violence Prevention Week,
Health Classes,
Fundraisers,
Response to a current event, such as a hate crime,
Church youth groups,
Summer camps,
One-act festivals,
…and any other place you can think of!

CHECKLIST OF THE PROCESS

You may be old-hand at putting together a show, but here are
the major steps to take:

- ✓ Choose your pieces!
- ✓ Start a notebook
- ✓ Get a cast, a venue, a rehearsal schedule, and copies of scripts
- ✓ Meet as a group, do group-building
- ✓ Rehearse, rehearse, rehearse!
- ✓ Assemble props and costumes
- ✓ Confirm venue, decide whether to have a talk-back
     or other type of post-show material
- ✓ Arrange for someone to be facilitator for post-performance talk-back
- ✓ Run-through
- ✓ Network with LGBTQ and Allied Organizations to be at the show
- ✓ Perform! Facilitate discussion/Collect Surveys!
- ✓ Review with cast about how it went
- ✓ Do it again!

DIRECTING 101

If you've not directed a show before, it's helpful to know what you are getting into. We've listed some tips to get you organized. Do what works for you.

TIP #1: A NOTEBOOK
The director's notebook is helpful for keeping everything organized.

Script, to-do lists, contact info, rehearsal schedule, notes for actors, and any details to keep your production on track. It doesn't have to be anything fancy.

TIP #2: SCHEDULING
Schedule what you can for mandatory rehearsals prior to auditions and rehearsals.

You may not be able to fill out a full rehearsal schedule until you know who is cast and what their schedules and conflicts will be (see the sample audition sheet), but, it is extremely helpful to know now whether or not people are available for the final dress rehearsals (where you will need everyone), and for the actual/potential performance dates. Find out when they are available.

TIP #3: CALL FOR ACTORS
Look outside your immediate circle.

Bringing in people you don't know can help identify and cultivate new allies. A call for actors might yield people who you would never have imagined would want to be part of this project. Here's a sample flyer or press release that you can send to newspapers, put around town, and on bulletin boards.

<u>Out & Allied AUDITIONS!!!</u>

Auditions and meeting will be held for Out & Allied
at USM Woodfords Campus Center in Portland, Maine
at **3pm on October 18, 2011**. Calling all young people,
ages 15-25 interested in being part of a performance
to create allies and support for LGBTQ youth.
Prepared audition monologues welcomed but not required.
To schedule an audition or FMI: Melanie at (207)555-4321

TIP #4-A: AUDITIONING
Be organized.
- Have an accessible, safe place to have the auditions.
- Consider scheduling people 3 or 4 at a time for a 20 minute block, so you can read people in different roles and start seeing pairings.
- Have multiple copies of script sections marked and labeled for easy access.
- Have someone outside of the audition space to check people in and have them fill out an audition sheet and stay with them while you (and maybe your assistant or co-director) work with others inside.

TIP #4-B: AUDITIONING
Don't do it.

It's quite possible to not have auditions at all. Perhaps you've got a club or group of people all interested already and they can choose their own roles.

TIP #5: CASTING
Follow your gut.

Effort vs. attitude vs. talent. If someone really wants to do something, let them in! The people you have to work hard to convince, or who always have an excuse, or who assume you'll bend over backwards for them are likely good for a headache in the future.
- Availability. If they're not free, there's no point!
- Enthusiasm. Look for it. If they don't want to do it don't force it.
- Team spirit. Huge egos don't usually get smaller, especially under pressure!
- Talent and capacity. You want your actors to have the ability to handle the role you want to cast them in.
- Comfort. Will the actor be okay with...*presenting to peers, possible bullies, authorities? Playing a character who is targeted as gay? The physical and verbal action of the scene, such as touching or being touched, yelling, the blocking? Memorizing their lines? Performing a solo monologue?*

TIP #6: CONTACT SHEETS
Make them, share them.

It seems obvious, but it's easy to overlook. Everyone—cast and crew—should have a copy. Include name, role or function, phone number, email address.

OUT & ALLIED AUDITION SHEET SAMPLE

Contact Information
Name:
Age:
Height:
Hair color:
Phone:
Email:

Schedule Information
Mark time slots when you are available with "OK", and put an X through times when you have a conflict. Please be flexible as much as possible so we can find times to meet as a group!

	Mon.	Tues.	Wed.	Thurs.	Fri.	Sat.	Sun.
9-12 am							
12-3 pm							
3-5 pm							
5-7 pm							

Dates & times of specific schedule conflicts:

Additional Information
Please list any previous acting experience (no worries if you don't have any yet—just say so!):

Why do you want to be a part of this project?

Would you object to being cast as a different gender or orientation? If so, please be specific.

REHEARSALS AND THE REHEARSAL PROCESS

WHAT DOES IT MEAN TO RUN A REHEARSAL?

Rehearsals tend to run 1 to 3 hours each, and you should have 2 to 4 per week, depending on your timeline and depending on whether actors will be on or off book for the performance. If you're working with a lot of people you might have just a few come at a time so you can focus on their scene—it may mean more time in rehearsals for the director, but it's not great to have people standing around. If you need to focus on just a couple of people for a bit, you can have the other actors run their lines or scenes out of the room. Even with breaking down and rehearsing just sections, be sure to make time for all-group rehearsals too! Of course, you could divide and conquer, and have a reader's theatre version ready in a snap.

THE BASICS:

Here's a list of questions…
- Is the space you rehearse in big enough to allow your cast to move around freely?
- If you can't use the stage you will actually be performing on, can you get measurements and tape on the floor the dimensions so the actors can get used to specific constraints?
- Do you have the basic props the actors need? (Don't wait—get actors used to handling items from the beginning.)
- If you are doing a staged reading, do you have music stands, podium, or microphone that the actors will need to practice with?
- If you are working with a newly written piece, have you built in time to give the piece a reading and a rough block of time for the playwright to make the changes that are nearly guaranteed to be needed? (see section about writing your own pieces)
- Is the order of the pieces working, or are double casting issues making transitions (for actor or for audience) tricky?

ON BOOK:

If you can't have everyone memorize lines, it is fine for the actors to carry scripts, depending on time constraints and the level of production. The choice should be uniform—if one person needs to carry it, probably all others should carry theirs as well. If people are working from scripts, whether reading at a podium or with full movement, you'll want to help the actors from the beginning get used to managing their hands and the eye contact needed with the audience... no one wants to look at the top of an actor's head. And, just because they are reading, it doesn't mean they should *sound like* they are reading!

OFF BOOK:

If you are doing a more polished performance, set a date—as early as possible, perhaps after the first or second blocking rehearsal—for the actors to be off book. Utilize an assistant or have actors share the responsibility of being "on book" so actors can call for lines as they make the full transition. Be a stickler for when you want them to be off book as well as for accuracy of lines: the fact is, actors cannot really do much work on the acting if they are only trying to remember what to say and where to be on stage.

- *Safe Space* – *Make this a place where no one feels put down or made to feel "less-than."*

- *Trust* – *feel like you don't have to question your fellow cast members – that you work as a group and no one gets let down.*

- *Confidentiality* – *what gets said here about personal experience and sharing stuff, STAYS HERE.*

- *Cooperation / Teamwork* – *everyone works together to build ideas and actions.*

HOW TO BLOW IT, SERVED THREE WAYS

HOW TO BLOW IT AS A DIRECTOR

Be completely self absorbed.
Come to rehearsal unprepared.
Be as uptight as possible. Yelling at actors also helps.
Encourage people to be late—or, better still, be late yourself!
Micromanage everything, because you *know* no one can be trusted to do their job.

> OR...There are lots of books to help you think like a director. But mostly it's a combination of vision, openness to discovery, and an ability to help people find their strengths. You are not the greatest in the group, but rather the one that allows everyone else to be great.

HOW TO DO TERRIBLE ACTIVISM

Assume you know what other people are thinking.
Assume that what's okay for you is okay for others.
Assume that what worked before will work the same way this time.
Assume that there will be no obstacles or change of plans.
Assume you know better or more than anyone else.

> OR...There is more than one way to be an activist, and not all strategies are created equal, and not all actions fit every individual. This is to say: trust yourself. You know what will work, and it is just fine to learn as you go. In fact, it's best to stay open to the possibility of things going differently. Assuming you already know everything will surely limit your effect as an activist, and probably get you on some peoples' bad side.

HOW TO KILL A PERFORMANCE

Perform so quietly that no one can hear the words.
Treat your audience like they are the enemy.
Treat your audience like they are dumb and can't think for themselves.

Forget that other people have their own stories about what it feels like to be alone, unwelcome, or disrespected.

Use shocking language so the audience will only focus on the shock-word/action rather than your overall message.

> OR...Each performance is a different entity unto itself—the audience is different, the actors have different energy from yesterday, and who knows what current event or bit of personal news is going to impact what happens today. Remember your reasons for choosing to perform. Be strong and let your audience be strong with you.

SHARE THE LOAD

- Advertise for actors
- Schedule a place for auditions
- Schedule/run auditions—or organize the meeting of like-minded folks
- Get actor schedules and conflicts (see sample audition sheet)
- Make company contact list (name, phone, email address)
- Secure date/time/place for first performance
- Work out the rehearsal schedule and a deadline for readying the show
- Secure rehearsal space
- Help each other run lines
- Assemble props and decide on costumes
- Create programs
- Invite the resource folks
- Secure a facilitator and panel
- Line up someone to distribute programs
- More? Yes! Fill in here:

TAKING THE SHOW ON THE ROAD

It takes a lot of work to put on a show. It's also hard to get an audience, if they aren't captive in a classroom or for an assembly. However, nearly every time the show has been presented, someone in the audience has said, "this needs to be seen at my_____! Can you perform there??" The answer might be no—and maybe some actors can't commit to another show, but just in case, prepare!

- What are the dimensions of the space, and are there any variations of levels?

- Where are the entrances and exits, how much room is off stage?

- Is there a place for the actors to prepare and safely leave their stuff?

- Can the venue provide the chairs and other set items you need, or do you have to bring them?

- How is everyone getting there?

- More? Yes! Fill in here:

PRODUCING
THE EVENT

THEATRE FOR CIVIC DIALOGUE
AND SOCIAL CHANGE

SPECIAL CONSIDERATIONS

- What will participation and visibility as LGBTQ-friendly
  mean for individuals in your production?
- Are there issues to be sensitive about, such as negative reactions
  from family or friends?
- In addition to your performers, will your work cause stress
  on LGBTQ folks in your audience?
- What can you do ahead of time and at the performance to ensure that
  people have access to the support and resources they may need?
- Have you identified someone to be an on-call support person
  to be on site if someone becomes upset and needs to talk?
  Are they comfortable or experienced in this capacity?

KNOW YOUR AUDIENCE

Because the pieces that you will be performing will bring up different things for different people, you want to be cautious when organizing what happens after the show. For some, they might not feel safe "outing" themselves, and therefore would be uncomfortable with a talk back that poses questions like "as a lesbian, do you think this performance did a good job showing the importance of allies?" That could make someone very uncomfortable and could create more problems than solutions.

What goes into your post show program?

- *Presentation by LGBTQ and Allied Organizations?*
- *Local violence prevention advocates?*
- *Respected community member support?*
- *Principal, clergy, school leaders?*
- *Cast member Q & A?*

Chances are that the folks who came to the show are already allies, or interested in knowing how to be better allies to the LGBTQ community. There might be the rare person in the back row being a hater, but most are there to listen and support. It has happened in the past that when someone from the audience asks "How can I help?" or "How can I be a better ally?" after the show, the cast has not known how to answer. Isn't that why we're performing in the first place? This would be something to discuss with the cast and crew before the show. How would everyone answer that question? How *can* people who come to the show help in the future?

EDITOR'S NOTE:

If you do have a talk-back where folks can come up
to a microphone and speak, be respectful, honor your
cast members as well as the audience, and keep a positive
atmosphere. If things happen to get heated up,
remind everyone that " this is a respectful dialogue. "

The Power of the Post-Show Discussion

Post-show discussions for LGBTQ material always involve the risk of homophobic responses, but the benefits far outweigh these risks. When I directed Performances from the Out & Allied Project, I told my actors to expect all sorts of questions and comments—both positive and negative—and made it clear that they did not have to answer any questions with which they were uncomfortable. I moderated each post-show discussion, fielding questions and turning them over to the actors. I strongly believe that including a post-show discussion with every performance of pieces from this collection is essential. Post-show discussions allow the audience to interact with the actors and director and ensure that everyone's voice is heard. This is the beginning of community-building. The post-show discussions for our production of Performances from the Out & Allied Project were amazing. One man stood up, pointed to an actor on stage, and said, on the verge of tears, "That is my son. He is gay. I am so proud of him." Another audience member volunteered, "I am the mother in 'After Breakfast.' That is my situation. I am working to understand my child and being here has given me a tremendous sense of community." At almost every post-show discussion, someone in the audience would ask the group of actors some form of the question, "So are you all gay?" I told the actors they could share their sexualities with the audience or choose not to do so. They all chose to identify themselves. Of the seventeen actors involved, two identified as gay and fifteen as straight. Audiences, especially high school audiences, were usually surprised. They wanted to know why straight actors would choose to play LGBTQ roles, the implication of which was that the actors might be perceived as gay. One female actor responded, "I didn't know a lot about LGBTQ experiences until I became involved with this project. Learning about LGBTQ issues has made me passionate about fighting for the rights of my friends, family, and even complete strangers who deserve equality and our respect." One of the most powerful moments occurred during a post-show discussion at a high school when an actor volunteered that he was a straight former U.S. Marine. The audience was, for a few brief seconds, quiet, shocked that a Marine would participate in the Out & Allied Project. But after those few suspenseful seconds, the entire auditorium erupted in applause for him. They respected his service to our country and his story made the Out & Allied Project more real to them. A teacher approached me just before our second performance at the high school and thanked me for bringing the show to the high school's students. She remarked that when she returned to her classroom after the first performance, some "big, really macho jock types" sat down in their seats and said simply, "Yeah, I know some gay people; it's no big deal." For this teacher, the response of these students was a welcomed change to the homophobic behavior she had witnessed in the past. The combination of the production and post-show discussion allowed the high school audience as well as the audiences for all of our performances to see the connections between the actors, the actors' characters, and the audiences' own real world experiences.

Meghan Brodie

ANATOMY OF A TALK-BACK

Not all performance situations are going to call for a formal or even an informal talk-back. However, if you do decide to have a talk-back, what you need is a facilitator.

Consider a facilitator to be a Must Have.

WHO SHOULD FACILITATE?

A facilitator is often a neutral, respected, and known-to-the-audience individual who is comfortable thinking on their feet, good at really listening to what people have to say, and is capable of holding order.

Determine who will be a good choice from your group—it could be the director, producer, one of the cast, or someone else, such as a counselor, community leader or administrator. Or it could be some combination of the above. There could be a variety of responses to the play, to which you and your actors can listen to and respond respectfully. Be prepared—responses will vary from group to group.

TALK-BACK TIPS FOR THE ACTORS:
- Try not to get defensive about what you did and why. If someone is being negative, it might be more about their discomfort than something that you should take personally.
- Listen. You just had 10 or 20 or 60 minutes of power. Say less, and maybe ask your audience questions!
- Thank people for sharing and asking their questions.
- If a question is too uncomfortable for you to answer, for whatever reason, you can just say "I'd rather not talk about that in this situation, but maybe I could answer another question for you?" (Be careful not to pass the question on to someone else!)
- If a question is sensitive or long, but you want to answer it, invite them to chat with you after the talk-back.
- Do not out anyone who does not wish to be outed—in fact, let people out themselves!
- Don't take it personally. (This is hard to do, so it bears repeating!)

TALK-BACK TIPS FOR THE FACILITATOR:
Your job is to manage a meaningful discussion, and to keep it safe and civil. Here are some general guidelines for facilitating.

- **Introduce the show:** The audience should know to stay after the performance. For those staying, they will meet the cast, or a panel of local resources, and discuss what they saw and felt.

- **Inform:** Let people know that if something comes up for them and they need someone to listen to them, there is a "safe person" to talk to one-on-one briefly outside of the room. (This could be one of the actors, a friend or a parent, someone from your panel of local resources, etc. Ask one of these people, *before* your performance, to help out in this manner if needed).

- **Transition:** Once the applause finishes at the end of the show, don't waste any time getting to the front to start the transition from the performance to the conversation. Announce that you will be starting the talk-back now. You can start by sharing what you were moved by in the performance (i.e., I was touched by the piece with the mother, because it reminded me of my sister and how difficult a time my mom had when she came out), and invite the audience to share their personal responses.

- **Manage:** Hold the reins for the flow of the conversation. Direct the questions; invite people to talk; repeat audience questions or comments so that the rest of the audience can hear before moving on; keep people on track; don't allow either a panelist or an audience member to hijack the discussion (this can be a delicate matter!); fill in with your own questions if it's too quiet.

- **Time:** If you have said "we'll chat for 15 minutes," note the time at 15 minutes, and then invite people who need to leave to do so. Ask for last comments. Invite people to mingle with the cast afterwards. You could serve refreshments or host a bake sale after the show.

- **THANK:** Thank the actors, writers, and director(s) for their work, thank the audience for their time and participation, and thank everyone for doing what they can to be better allies.

SUGGESTED DISCUSSION QUESTIONS

1. What are your responses to this performance? Observations? Highlights?

2. What do you think the writers, actors and director(s) wanted to achieve?

3. What do you see differently, or what do you now see as possible after seeing this performance?

4. What will you take away from this performance?

5. How do you see your community being supportive of the LGBTQ community, and how might these communities become better allies?

6. What does it mean to be an ally?

7. Others?

EMMY'S TIPS FOR STAGING CHANGE

• Clearly define roles – actors, director(s), stage manager, lights, costumes, etc. Make sure everyone is okay with the way that things have been divided up before starting. Moving forward is much easier if at the beginning everyone is on the same page, knows clearly what is expected of them specifically, and honors the roles and responsibilities that others have taken on.

• Get to know each other. Have a cast party at the beginning *and* at the end of the show! This can be a personal experience, and can be fun.

• Play to your audience. Depending on where you stage your show, it will be received differently. Middle school students will react differently than college students, and attitudes and sensitivity may be heightened due to a recent event or community tension.

• Your post-show action is important. A lot of emotion is stirred up with performances, especially when the show is designed to communicate and incite action. Having a talk-back, or giving people some direction and support after the show can mean the difference between someone getting depressed and going home feeling alone and overwhelmed, to someone being inspired and rushing up to the cast and crew or the supporting organizations eager to talk more about what's next and what they can do! Support your audience as they support you.

• That being said, you are not the experts. Make the talk-back and actions that follow the show inclusive, and be open to what the specific people in the room have to say. You never know what could result from what you do—invite miracles!

Emmy Raviv

WRITING

GETTING STARTED WRITING
A PRODUCTION-WORTHY PIECE

Pick up a pen and paper. Sit down with a computer. Find a favorite chair, brew a cup of tea, light a candle—whatever you need to get your ideas out. The best way to write is to start writing. Here are some prompts to get you started, or give you ideas as you go along:

- Tell about a time when you were really proud...
- Tell about a time when you were really angry, upset or disappointed...
- Tell about a time you/someone else made a choice to come out...
- What did you wish someone had told you about identifying as LGBTQ?
- Tell about how it feels to love or be friends with someone who is LGBTQ...
- Write about being an educated ally…
- Start with a moment in which you stepped up to support someone (or you didn't)…
- Share a time when you expected one response from someone, and got something else entirely—good or bad…

What do you do with a prompt?
Pick one! Or maybe it inspires another one. Regardless, try some of these writing strategies:

- Go. Don't put your pen down or stop at the keyboard for a set amount of time, ignoring all spelling and repetition and nonsense. Three minutes? Ten minutes? Twenty? Then, read it out loud and see what you've got.
- Start with a question. Stuck? Ask. Then ask more questions, either in the voice of the character, or in your voice to the character. You'll be amazed at how much this will open up. (This is also a good technique to do after you've drafted a piece, to see if you can dig down further and bring different layers to your characters and scenes.)
- Let it morph. Maybe you've got a scene you are trying to write but instead something else comes out. This is a good thing! Work with what comes, and go back to other things later.
- Talk through the prompt with friends or co-writers. Then go write.
- Improvisation! Get the creative flow with round robins, freeze games, free association. Do a hot seat for a character: grill the actor, who stays in character, with questions. It's a good way to find a natural voice and discover their funny & quirky side.
- More improv—after a scene is started or stuck, ask co-writers or actors to tell the story from another character's perspective.

Still Stuck?

Pick a time and place, name your characters as they appear. You can always go back and change them, but giving them a name right away can help ground them and help you get to know them. You could write about...

Having a crush • Buying clothes • Bending gender •
Applying for a Job • Meeting someone who you thought would be
an enemy but became a friend • Helping a sibling or friend who
is at their edge • Expecting support or something scary to happen
and getting/not getting what you expected • Getting through a day at school •
Getting through a holiday with family • A first (or last!) date •
Visiting the doctor • Being in a locker room or public rest room •
Knowing a friend or family member is not heterosexual but they don't yet,
or haven't yet come out • Overhearing someone use the word "gay"
or "queer" in a derogatory or hateful way • Bi-sexuality as a "trend" •
Challenging the definitions of "sexuality" and "spirituality"

Revise.

There may be a few of you out there who are able to write from your head to the page perfectly in one go. It happens. Most of the time writers have false starts, and write pages before they find the one paragraph they were after. They know their writing is "awesome" and "clever" and "perfect," until an actor or friend reads it out loud. Here are some questions that can help you make your work better.

Ask yourself:

- Are the stakes high enough? What could make it more intense?
- Why are these actions/responses/events happening today?
- Is there a way to keep it real but ALSO increase the dramatic impact? Or, conversely, is there a way to make it less real to soften the hardness of a true moment so people can actually hear it?
- Can I interject humor at an awkward moment, or just before or after a heavy moment?
- If based on a true situation, are there places I can eliminate details because they aren't helping to move the piece forward?
- Are there details I can add that would make the moment even more specific, and in turn, serve to make the character even more complete and complex?
- Is there something competing with my most important point?
- Is there anything having an unintended impact?
- Is there a sense of a journey in the piece?

And Revise Again.

Read out loud, make changes, and then have someone else read it out loud. You may need to ask the actor to read and try some of the action to see if it works. There is nothing that will send you more cheerfully back to the draft than listening to an actor stumbling over your awkward sentences, or seeing a joke fall flat, or recognizing that what was perfectly clear in your mind in fact needs more explanation. Sometimes a reading will help you find an ending, fix a scene that's not working, or navigate the emotions of the piece better. Actors and readers love to share their thoughts with you.

It's best to avoid the death question: "Do you like it?" You are creative; ask better questions! Here are a few:
- What do you like about this piece?
- What is not making sense to you?
- Is there anything that you'd like more information about?
- I'm interested in how the _____ is coming across. What do you think about that part of the piece?
- What does the piece leave you thinking, wondering, feeling?

Content Questions

Language issues? Whatever colorful term you want to use might be realistic to the scene, and, it might be a distraction from what you are trying to do. Theatre is not real life, but can reflect reality. Often the f-bombs and shocking stuff isn't actually all that necessary— except when it is. It seems there are always exceptions to every rule. You'll have to be the judge, and your audience/performance situation might dictate how to resolve this. (add**verb** may or may not be able to publish or put on the website, however, if that matters to you.)

Showing the bully or hate on stage? Mostly we know what these people look like, and don't need a refresher. What is more interesting is what people do about it, how it makes them feel, and what the result is.

Using stereotypes? Stereotypes are, well, stereotypical, and generally they are not very nice or helpful. It's good to imagine what someone of the stereotype you are working with would think of your characterization. Will it insult? Alienate? Shut down conversation?

Here are some thoughts about language from an Out & Allied director:

Directing ten pieces from this anthology was an incredibly rewarding artistic endeavor, but it was also an excellent educational experience. Working with college and high school students, many of whom identified as straight, provided me with an opportunity to foster conversations about queer identity, beginning, appropriately enough, with one about the word "queer." Students asked, "Is queer an offensive term? When is it okay to use the word queer?" We discussed the reclamation of the once (and for some, still) offensive term by queer communities and the manner in which it currently functions as an umbrella term to describe a variety of combinations of sex, gender, and sexuality. And when a student referred to a male friend as a "homosexual" during a post-show discussion, we were able to explore why "gay" was a less clinical, more appropriate choice for some. Similarly, we clarified the differences between "transgender" and "transsexual" and talked about the power of language and the challenges it can pose to community building. The pieces that constituted our production of performances from the Out & Allied Project used a vast array of terms to describe a broad range of identities and prompted everyone involved with the production to consider how we understand ourselves and relate to those around us in respectful and meaningful ways.

Meghan Brodie

And one more time, revise.
Invariably, the work the actors and directors do will add more specific changes though the production process. Be sure to capture these for your final copy.

If you want to submit your work to add**verb** for publication, either in a book or on the website, please send a copy of your piece, with title and author credit instructions with the release form (found next in the book, or on the website, www.addverbproductions.org).

We strongly encourage you to send it along, as OUT & ALLIED: 2nd EDITION is on its way!

HAPPY WRITING!

Agreement
(Author 18 Years or Older)

Name of Author: _____
(please print or type author's name)

Submission: _____
(please print or type title of the Submission)

Date: _____
(please print or type today's date)

For value received, the above identified author hereby transfers and irrevocably assigns to add**verb** Productions Art and Education ("add**verb**") the above-titled Submission, along with any and all copyrights and other intellectual property rights in and to the Submission.

Author represents that s/he is 18 years of age or older and that the Submission was his/her original creation and that no other party has any rights or interests in the Submission. Author agrees that add**verb** may use the Submission in any manner and for any purpose it deems appropriate without further consent from or obligation to Author.

Author further agrees that s/he will sign any documents and take any actions reasonably required by add**verb** to confirm add**verb's** title to and ownership of the Submission and all intellectual property rights therein.

To the extent that add**verb** deems it appropriate to provide Author with authorship credit, such credit will be provided as follows: _____
_____
(please print or type form of credit to be provided or leave blank or write "anonymous" if no credit is desired)

☐ This piece has been produced/in print in the past
   (please check if correct)

If so, please explain: _____
_____
_____

Seen and agreed to as of the date stated above by:

_____   _____
(print your name)   *(sign/signature)*

Agreement
(Author Not 18 Years or Older)

Name of Child Author: _____
(please print or type author's name)

Name/Relation of Parent/Guardian: _____
(please print or type parent/guardian relationship and name)

Submission: _____
(please print or type title of the Submission)

Date: _____
(please print or type today's date)

For value received, the above-identified parent/guardian of the above-identified
Child Author hereby transfers and irrevocably assigns to add**verb** Productions Art
and Education ("add**verb**") on behalf of such Child Author the above-titled Submission, along
with any and all copyrights and other intellectual property
rights in and to the Submission.

The above-identified parent/guardian represents that s/he is the parent/legal guardian of the Child
Author and that, to the best of his/her knowledge, the Submission was the Child Author's original
creation and that no other party has any rights or interests in the Submission. The above-identified
parent/guardian agrees that add**verb** may use the Submission in any manner and for any purpose it
deems appropriate without further consent from or obligation to him/her or the Child Author.

The above-identified parent/guardian further agrees that s/he will sign any documents and take
any actions reasonably required by add**verb** to confirm add**verb's** title to and ownership of the
Submission and all intellectual property rights therein.

To the extent that add**verb** deems it appropriate to provide Child Author
with authorship credit, such credit will be provided as follows: _____

_____
*(please print or type form of credit to be provided or leave blank or write "anonymous" if
no credit is desired)*

☐ This piece has been produced/in print in the past
    (please check if correct)

If so, please explain: _____
_____
_____

Seen and agreed to as of the date stated above by:

_____
(print your name)   *(sign/signature)*

LEADERSHIP

Your leadership matters. Who knows, you might even win a Presidential Award. But the truth is, you don't need an award to recognize when you've made a difference in someone's life. You know it because it comes with a good, warm, & humble feeling at your core.

"Everyone involved with the 2010 production of Performances from the Out & Allied Project knowingly participated in a form of social activism. The actors and writers were fearless. They saw injustice in the world around them and made a conscious decision to change the world because change is possible. The pieces in this volume detail a wide array of experiences with humor, compassion, and fire and reflect a sincere desire to be heard and cultivate allies. The work of everyone associated with the Out & Allied Project continues to move me and I hope you find inspiration in the stories collected here."

Meghan Brodie

INTERVIEW WITH DANIELLE SMITH

Interviewed by Micah Malenfant, June 2010

Photo courtesy GLSEN

Danielle Smith has been an inspirational advocate for gay rights and an ally of the LGBTQ community for years, and is only 18. The same year that she graduated as Valedictorian from Mt. Ararat High School in Topsham, Me., 2010, Danielle was also the recipient of GLSEN's Student Advocate of the Year Award. She served as the Jump Start leader for GLSEN's Southern Maine Chapter, as well as her high school's GSA President. Before she visited Washington D.C. to receive her award from President Obama personally, we had the chance to interview her, and hope that you find her words and her work an encouragement to your own.

Micah Malenfant: Where does your passion come from? (Considering there are millions of straight individuals in the world who remain indifferent towards these issues).

Danielle Smith: This is hard for me to pinpoint exactly...ever since I can remember I have had a really strong sense of justice and a passion for equality. My parents are not exactly civil rights activists, but they did raise me to believe that everyone has inherent worth and dignity and that everyone should be treated fairly. I think that LGBTQ activism is my main outlet for that passion. After all, this is the civil rights movement of the present! We'll be in the history books someday. When I was in 8th grade I became good friends with the president of my high school's Gay Straight Alliance. He told me about the group and I became involved in 9th grade. Everything has spiraled out of control (but in a good way, haha) from there.

MM: Were there moments when it was hard to be an advocate?

DS: Oh, absolutely. As a member of the majority group it is so easy to put your head down and try to forget about discrimination. Over the years I've experienced direct opposition to the Day of Silence from students who organized a Straight Day. It is STILL hard for me to stand up to peers when I hear them use anti-gay language. It's a scary and intimidating thing to do with people you don't know very well. But you have to get over that...This is something that I have to do for my own personal conscience and for the well being of those around me. I can't stand by and watch my friends and family members get harassed or be discriminated against.

MM: Have you ever been labeled solely based on the fact that you stood up for gays and lesbians?

DS: People that don't know me well often assume that I'm lesbian, but I just politely correct them. I'm not offended by it at all, after all, in my view it's not a bad thing to be a lesbian! I had a pretty visible and long term heterosexual relationship in high school, so I never really experienced harassment or discrimination based on assumptions that I was gay.

MM: In doing all of this work, what is your hope for the future?

DS: I want to be able to walk into the high school of my son or daughter or niece or nephew and not hear the phrase "that's so gay." I want a world without bullying. I want Gay Straight Alliances to become unnecessary. I guess those are pretty lofty goals, but I believe we're headed in that direction.

MM: Why is it important for straight individuals to be allies?

DS: Straight allies are SO IMPORTANT. I cannot stress that enough. History shows that no oppressed group has ever truly overcome their oppression without help from concerned people in the majority group. No civil rights movement has ever succeeded without allies. When straight allies fight for gay equality, and are out and open about their heterosexuality, it removes the stigma from LGBTQ activism work. Twenty years ago, involvement in this work automatically labeled you as gay. Today, that is not the case— straight allies are visible and numerous. This trend needs to continue for our civil rights movement's success.

MM: Your work was done in a rural, small town community. How did this effect the movement?

DS: I'm very fortunate to live in the liberal northeast, but living in a rural area has definitely affected my work. As the recent marriage vote shows, Maine is incredibly divided. Northern Maine and rural areas are very, very conservative, while the southern half of the state and the more urban areas are very liberal. Unfortunately, I live in a rural town without much support (Bowdoin went 70/30 against marriage equality). Fortunately, I live within a 10 minute drive of Brunswick (which went 60/40 in favor) and a 40 minute drive of Portland (70/30 in favor). My school community consists of four towns, two of which are mostly liberal and two of which are fairly conservative. It certainly makes for an interesting school climate, and as a result I've experienced both lavish support and direct opposition to my work. I like to think that over the past four years the acceptance and support has increased, however.

MM: How do you plan to keep being an activist as you go onto college at Dartmouth?

DS: All of the schools I applied to had a Gay Straight Alliance of some sort. It was a requirement for me. Dartmouth has a fantastic one called Gender, Sexuality XYZ. After I had applied, the admissions office sent me a link to a video chat with the co-presidents of the group because of the activism that they saw in my application. That's how awesome Dartmouth is. Also, I visited during Pride week, so I got to meet the group and see their space and hear someone from the Gay and Lesbian Victory Fund speak. There was even a rainbow flag up on the outside of the student center. I am so looking forward to joining the group and continuing my activism at Dartmouth.

MM: What are your three reasons to be an ally?

DS: 1) You're helping to achieve equality—what could be more rewarding that that?!
2) You'll meet amazing and inspiring people.
3) And, best of all, it's really fun!

THE RIGHT TO ESTABLISH A GSA

IN PUBLIC SCHOOLS: A BASIC PRIMER

Prepared by GLAD (Gay and Lesbian Advocates & Defenders)
July 2010 // www.glad.org

Can a school refuse to allow the establishment of a GSA?

Under the Equal Access Act, which is a federal law, any school that permits non-curriculum related student groups must provide equal access to all student groups, and that includes equal access for GSAs. Equal access means that the GSA must be afforded all the same rights and privileges as other student groups to use the facilities at the school for meetings and communications.

The text of the Equal Access Act, found at 20 U.S.C. § 4071(a), reads as follows:

It shall be unlawful for any public secondary school which receives Federal financial assistance and which has a limited open forum to deny equal access or a fair opportunity to, or discriminate against, any students who wish to conduct a meeting within that limited open forum on the basis of the religious, political, philosophical, or other content of the speech at such meetings.

The United States Supreme Court has been crystal clear that the EAA requires schools "to grant equal access to student groups." Bd of Educ. Of Westside Comm. Sch. v. Mergens, 496 U.S. 226, 237 (1900). A school is subject to the EAA if it: (1) receives federal financial assistance and, (2) has a "limited open forum."

What's a limited open forum?

A "limited open forum" exists if the school "grants an offering to or opportunity for one or more non-curriculum related student groups to meet on school premises during non-instructional time." This definition is drawn directly from the text of the EAA. The bottom line is that if any non-curriculum student groups are allowed to meet at a school that receives federal funds (which means any public school), then a GSA must be allowed to do so on the same terms.

What's the difference between a curriculum and a non-curriculum related group?

GSAs are typically "non-curriculum" related student groups. You can distinguish between a curriculum related school group and a non-curriculum related group using the following examples. In a school that teaches French language, the French Club would be considered a curriculum related group. Similarly, all schools teach Math and therefore the Math Club would be a curriculum related group.

Meanwhile, common non-curriculum groups include the Skating Club, Asian club, Black Student Union, Christian Club, Key Club, Scuba Diving Club and Chess Club. GSAs fall within this category of school clubs.

As long as a school accepts federal funding and has at least one non-curriculum related student group that meets during non-instructional time, the EAA prohibits the school from disallowing the GSA to do the same.

Can a school force a GSA to have a different name of purpose?

It is well-established that a school cannot require a GSA to adopt another name such as the "Diversity Club" or the "Tolerance Club," nor can it force a GSA to broaden its scope beyond the reach of LGBTQ issues. Refusal to allow students to form a GSA on the ground that the group must have a different name, or that it must have a different purpose, violates the Equal Access Act. Because other non-curricular groups are not forced to change their name or their purpose, for a school to force or attempt to force a GSA to do so would constitute impermissible differential treatment under the EEA.

There have been several court cases involving schools that have tried to force GSAs to adopt "less divisive" names or broaden the scope of the group's mission statement to include other issues. In all those cases, the GSAs have won the right to keep their name and their mission and the courts have found that it is impermissible for a school board to condition approval of the establishment of a GSA on a name change.

A GSA may choose to broaden its scope to include other issues, or it may vary its name if it chooses, but it cannot be forced by the school administration to do either.

Are there any legitimate bases for a school to deny a GSA?

There are two bases on which a school that allows other non-curricular groups may legitimately deny the formation of a GSA:

❶   Schools may exclude GSAs that do not comply with their club-formation policies, as long as those policies are evenly applied and not used as a pretext for discrimination.

Schools generally have rules for club formation. To be legitimate, the rules must be "content-neutral" - not aimed at the club's matter or constituents - but appropriately directed at procedure for forming and maintaining a club. For example, if a school has a policy that every group must have a faculty advisor, and if the school consistently enforces that policy, then that counts as a "content-neutral" rule. Thus, the failure of a GSA to identify a faculty advisor could be a legitimate reason for a school to deny a GSA. However, once a faculty advisor is found the group must be allowed to go forward.

In a case where this is an issue, it will be important to really analyze the school's policy and to understand the facts. Does every other non-curricular group have an advisor? Does the policy actually state that without an advisor the group cannot exist at all? What happens if there are temporary gaps in the advisor post (for example, a faculty member leaves or resigns his or her post and there is a lag before the new one is appointed). This may vary from school to school, so we will want to learn more fact when we hear that a group is encountering this problem.

It is important to note that the EAA is silent on the question of faculty advisors. This means that the law neither mandates nor prohibits them; schools are free to have a policy requiring a faculty advisor and we know that many schools do.

If a school has such a rule, or any other rule regarding club formation, and it is not consistently enforced, or not in a written policy accessible to students and faculty, some courts have concluded that the real reason for excluding the group was not its failure to follow the club formation rules but that, instead, the school was using that reason as a "pretext" for discriminating against the GSA.

❷ The EAA's Safe Harbor Provision

The EAA contains a safe harbor provision that allows a school to make distinctions among groups if necessary "to maintain order and discipline on school premises, to protect the well-being of students and faculty, and to assure that attendance of students at meetings is voluntary." As you might imagine, many school districts have invoked this safe harbor language in court to defend their refusal to recognize GSAs, arguing either that the presence of a GSA on campus would create uproar at the school and within the community, or that the presence of a GSA on campus would expose students to inappropriate messages.

In virtually all of these cases, the students have won and the schools have lost. This means that the courts have not, by and large, allowed schools to deny GSAs on the basis that they will be disruptive or will negatively affect student well-being. There has been just one exception, from a case in Texas, and that case had unique facts. For one thing, the GSA group in that case made explicit its commitment to teaching about safer sex in a school environment where the entire district had a formal abstinence-only policy. Additionally, the GSA there maintained its own web site on which it included a link to a very sexually explicit web site. Other cases around the country have distinguished this single case from Texas by pointing at its unique facts.

CONCLUSION

The great news is that student and advocates have strong arguments against schools that try to deny their right to form a GSA. The prevailing law favors the students wishing to form the GSA, not the schools trying to shut them down or keep them from getting established.

A school presented with this information should quickly understand that it must allow a GSA to form and exist on the same terms as other non-curricular clubs. However, should legal action become necessary, we can feel confident because cases challenging a school's refusal to allow a GSA have been overwhelmingly successful.

Here is a list of some of those successful GSA cases: Straights v. Osseo, 471 F.3d 908 (8th Cir. 2006); Gay-Straight Alliance of Yullee High Sch. Bd. of Nassau County, 602 F. Supp. 2d 1233 (M.D. Fl. 2009); Gonzalez v. Sch. Bd. of Okeechobee County, 571 F. Supp. 2d 1257 (S.D. Fl. 2008); Gay-Straight Alliance v. Sch. Bd. of Okeechobee, 483 F. Supp. 2d 1224 (S.D. Fl. 2007); White County High Sch. Peers in Diverse Educ. v. White County Sch. Dist., 2006 WL 1991990 (N.D. Ga. 2006); Boyd County High Sch. Gay Straight Alliance v. Bd. of Educ. Of Boyd County, 258 F. Supp. 2d 667 (E.D. Ky. 2003); Franklin Cent. Gay/Straight Alliance, 2002 WL 32097530 (S.D. Ind. 2002); East High Sch. PRISM Club v. Seidel, 95 F. Supp. 2d 1239 (D. Utah 2000); Colin v. Orange Unified Sch. Dist., 83 F Supp. 2d 1135 (C.D. Cal. 2000); East High Gay/Straight Alliance v. Bd. of Educ. Of Salt Lake City Sch. Dist., 81 F. Supp. 2d 1166 (D. Utah 1999).

GLOSSARY OF LGBTQ-RELATED TERMS

The glossary is designed to provide basic definitions of words and phrases commonly used in discussions sex, gender, and sexuality related issues. All language is constantly evolving; new terms are introduced, while others fade from use or change in meaning over time. The same word may mean different things to different people. It is always a good idea to respect the manner in which someone choses to self identify and the language that person prefers.

Ally: A member of the majority or dominant group who works to end oppression by supporting or advocating for the oppressed population. For example, any non-LGBTQ person who supports and stands up for the equality of LGBTQ people, sometimes referred to as a "straight ally," or, an adult who supports LGBTQ youth.

Androgynous: Having the characteristics or nature of both masculinity and femininity.

Asexual: A person who does not feel sexual attraction to anyone.

Biphobia: Fear of or aversion to bisexuality or bisexual people.

Bisexual: A sexual orientation and/or identity of a person who is sexually and emotionally attracted to some males and some females.

Cisgender: Refers to people whose gender identity and expression are aligned with their sex assigned at birth.

Coming Out: Declaring one's identity, specifically, being lesbian, gay, bisexual or transgender, whether to a person in private or a group of people. To be "in the closet" means to hide one's identity.

Drag: The theatrical performance of one or more genders, often involving the presentation of exaggerated, stereotypical gender characteristics.

Dyke: Derogatory term for a lesbian. Origin uncertain. Literally a dam or a bank, it could be a sexual reference to blocking a passage. Or it could come from "buildyker" a dam-builder, referring to a macho stereotype. Some lesbians have reclaimed the term and use it as an affirmation.

Equality: The concept that all people should be treated as equals and be given the same political, economic, social, and civil rights.

Equal Opportunities: The concept that everyone should have equal access to jobs, services, housing, medical care etc. whatever their race, ability, age, sexual orientation, gender, etc.

Faggot; Fag: A derogatory term for a gay or bisexual man (or sometimes any queer person). Literally a bundle of sticks that fuel a fire. Thought to relate to a medieval tradition of throwing 'sodomites' onto the fire whilst burning convicted criminals at the stake as a form of execution.

Family of Choice: Persons or group of people an individual sees as significant in their life. It may include none, all, or some members of their family of origin. In addition, it may include individuals such as significant others, domestic partners, friends, and coworkers.

FTM or F2M (female-to-male): An identity of a person who was assigned female at birth, and who identifies as male.

Gay: A sexual orientation and/or identity of a person who is sexually and emotionally attracted to some members of the same sex. Although gay can refer to both males and females, many prefer the term "lesbian" for females. Gay is sometimes used as an umbrella term to refer to all lesbian, gay and bisexual people, but some prefer the more inclusive term "LGBTQ" or "queer."

Gender: A social construct based on a group of emotional, behavioral, and cultural characteristics often referred to as feminine, masculine, androgynous, or other. Gender can be understood to have several components, including gender identity, gender expression, and gender role.

Gender Binary: The concept there are two genders: man and woman and a person must identify as either/or.

Gender Expression: The manner in which people express their gender identity through appearance, dress, mannerisms, speech patterns, and social interactions.

Gender Identity: How we identify ourselves in terms of our gender. Identities may be: male, female, androgynous, transgender and others.

Gender-Neutral Pronoun: A pronoun that does not associate a gender with the person being discussed. Two of the most common gender-neutral pronouns are "zie" (xe, ze) replacing she and he, and "hir" (xem, zir) replacing her and him. Some people choose to use "they" and "them" as singular pronouns to avoid gender identification.

Gender Non-Conforming or Gender Variant: An identity of a person who does not conform to traditional or societal binary gender expectations.

Gender Orientation: Individuals internal sense of their gender. Gender orientation doesn't necessarily align with the sex assigned at birth.

Gender Role: The social expectations of how an individual should act, think and/or feel based upon one's assigned biological sex. A set of traditional and stereotypical roles, traits, dress, characteristics, qualities, mannerisms and behaviors that are associated with soci- etal norms of masculine men and feminine females.

Genderism: The systematic belief that there are only two genders: men and women and that masculinity is attached to male bodies and femininity is attached to female bodies.

Genderqueer: An identity of people who identify as and/or express themselves as somewhere in the continuum between masculinity and femininity or outside of the gender binary system. Genderqueer people may or may not identify as LGBT.

Heterosexism: Applies to attitudes, bias, and discrimination in favor of heterosexuality and relationships. It includes the presumption that everyone is heterosexual or that male/female attractions and relationships are the norm and therefore superior. It is the belief that everyone is or should be straight.

Heterosexual: A sexual orientation and/or identity of a person who is sexually and emotionally attracted to some members of another sex (specifically, a male who is attracted to some females or a female who is attracted to some males). Often referred to as "straight."

Homophobia: Fear of or aversion to homosexuality or lesbian, gay or bisexual people.

Homosexual: An identity of people who are sexually and emotionally attracted to some members of their own sex; originated in the medical and psychological professions. Currently, many prefer the term lesbian or gay.

Institutional Oppression: Arrangement of a society used to benefit one group at the expense of another through the use of language, media education, religion, economics, etc.

Internalized Oppression: The process by which an oppressed person comes to believe, accept, or live out the inaccurate stereotypes and misinformation about their group.

Intersex: A general term used for a person born with reproductive or sexual anatomy that doesn't seem to fit the typical definitions of female or male. Intersex variances can affect the genitals, the chromosomes, and/or secondary sex characteristics.

Lambda: The Gay Activist Alliance originally chose the lambda, the Greek letter "L", as a symbol in 1970. Organizers chose the letter "L" to signify liberation. The word has become a way of expressing the concept "lesbian and gay male" in a minimum of syllables and has been adopted by such organizations as Lambda Legal Defense and Education Fund.

Lesbian: A sexual orientation and/or identity of a person who is female-identified and who is sexually and emotionally attracted to some other females.

LGBTQ: An umbrella term referring collectively to people who identify as lesbian, gay, bisexual and/or transgender, those who identify as questioning and/or queer, intersex, asexual, and more. The "+" is a symbol of inclusivity for those who do not identify as L,G,B,T,Q,I, or A. In the past "gay" was used as a general, overar- ching term, but currently the more inclusive terms LGBT, LGBTQ, and LGBTQIA+ are regularly used and preferred by many LGBTQ people and allies. The word "queer" is also frequently used as an umbrella term to include a wide range of sex, genders, and sexuality combinations.

MTF or M2F (male-to-female): An identity of a person who was assigned male at birth, and who identifies as female.

Non-Op: A trans-identified person whose identity does not involve receiving Sexual Reassignment Surgery/Sex Confirmation Surgery.

On T: When a person takes the hormone testosterone.

Pansexual: A sexual orientation and/or identity of a person who is sexually and emotionally attracted to people regardless of their gender expression and/or identity.

Post-Op: A trans-identified person who has received Sexual Reassignment Surgery/Sex Confirmation Surgery.

Pre-Op: A trans-identified person who has not received Sexual Reassignment Surgery; implies that the person does intend to receive such surgical procedures.

Pride: An affirmation of one's self and the LGBTQ community as a whole. The modern 'pride' movement began after the Stonewall riots in 1969. Pride marches are common in western societies.

Queer: An umbrella term used to describe a sexual orientation, gender identity, or gender expression that does not conform to heteronormative society. While it is used as a neutral, or even a positive term among many LGBTQ people today, historically it has been used negatively and is still considered derogatory by many.

Questioning: An identity of people who are uncertain of their sexual orientation and/or identity and/or their gender identity.

Sex or Biological Sex: This can be considered our "packaging" and is determined by our chromosomes (often XX or XY), our hormones, and our internal and external genitalia. Typically, we are assigned the sex of male or female at birth, though some are born intersex.

Sex Reassignment Surgery (SRS)/Sex Confirmation Surgery: A term used by some medical professionals to refer to a group of surgical options that alter a person's sex to match their sex identity.

Sexual Behavior: What we do sexually and with whom.

Sexual Identity: What we call ourselves in terms of our sexuality. Such labels include "lesbian," "gay," "bisexual," "queer," "heterosexual," "straight," among many more.

Sexual Orientation: A person's emotional and/or sexual attraction toward others.

Sodomy; Sodomy laws: Anal or oral copulation with a member of the same or opposite sex. Derived from the story of Sodom and Gommorah, in the book of Genesis. Historically used to selectively persecute gay people. These were ruled unconstitutional by the U.S Supreme Court in *Lawrence v. Texas* (2003).

Stereotype: A set of overly simplistic generalizations about a group of people that allows others to categorize them and treat them accordingly.

Transgender: An identity of people whose gender identity is not aligned with their sex assigned at birth and/or whose gender expression is non-conforming.

Transition: The variety of actions a person may take to transition from one gender/sex identity to another. These may include social, psychological and/or medical processes. Transitioning is a complex process that occurs over a long period of time, not a one-time event.

Transphobia: Fear of or aversion to transgender people or those who are perceived to break or blur societal norms regarding gender identity or gender expression.

Transsexual: A term, originated in medical and psychological communities, that historically referred to people whose gender identity was not aligned with their sex assigned at birth.

Triangle: A symbol of remembrance. Gay men in the Nazi concentration camps were forced to wear the pink triangle as a designation of being homosexual Women who did not conform to social roles, often believed to be lesbians, had to wear the black triangle. The triangles are worn today as symbols of freedom, reminding us to never forget.

Two-Spirit (also Two Spirit or Twospirit): Used in many Native American communities to refer to people who are lesbian, gay, bisexual, transgender or gender non-conforming. The term usually implies a masculine spirit and a feminine spirit living in the same body and has been adopted by some contemporary lesbian, gay, bisexual and transgender Native Americans to describe themselves.

Ze: Gender neutral pronouns that can be used instead of he/she.

Zir: Gender neutral pronouns that can be used instead of his/her.

This glossary was compiled from the Gay, Lesbian, and Straight Education Network's (GLSEN) Safe Space Kit; The Wateville Inclusive Community Project's Stand Up Action Toolkit; The GLAAD Media Reference Guide; the Rainbow Project; and the UC Berkeley Gender Equity Resource Center.

IDENTITY SPECTRUMS

SOURCE: www.translategender.org

SEX:

← —————————— intersex —————————— →

female   male

GENDER:

← —————————— gender queer —————————— →

woman   man

GENDER EXPRESSION:

← —————————— androgynous —————————— →

feminine   masculine

SEXUALITY:

← —————————— bisexual —————————— →

attracted to   pansexual   attracted to
male/masculine   asexual   female/feminine

LGBTQ
YOUTH THEATRE

add**verb's** *next anthology will include more writing from theatres that work specifically with LGBTQ youth. You may have noticed that we included several from That Uppity Theatre Company and its program Apple Pie. In the spirit of knowing what's going on out there in the world, here's a little more about this company and a letter from the founder, Joan Lipkin. There's also a Q+A session with Brian Guerhing of the Rose Theatre and The Pride Players, and a list of LGBTQ youth theatres and theatre projects around the country. There's a lot going on!*

Maybe you will be inspired to start your own company?

THAT UPPITY THEATRE COMPANY & APPLE PIE

That Uppity Theatre Company was founded by Joan Lipkin in 1989 to put the principles of cultural diversity into innovative theatrical practice and to promote civic dialogue and related activities. They specialize in working with underserved populations including LGBTQ youth, adults and their families, people with disabilities, women with cancer, urban youth, and adults with Alzheimers and early onset dementia to help develop their voices, create performances, and foster community. They are based in St. Louis and also do work in other parts of the country.

They have received numerous awards for their work including the Community Enhancement Award from the Human Rights Campaign, the What's Right with the Region for Promoting Racial Justice and Social Equality Award from Focus, the Brotherhood Sisterhood Award from the National Conference for Community and Justice, the John Van Voris Award from Pride St. Louis and a Visionary Award, among others.

That Uppity Theatre Company created "Apple Pie," a project with LGBTQ and allied youth in St. Louis several years ago, in partnership with Growing American Youth, one of the country's longest continuous support groups for youth. All are welcome, and no theatrical experience is necessary. Participants in Apple Pie are youth who have identified as lesbian, gay, bisexual, transgendered, intersex or allied. Three pieces included in this anthology have been written and performed as part of Apple Pie. For more info on That Uppity Theatre Company and Apple Pie, check them out online at www.uppityco.com.

A LETTER FROM SOMEONE WHO'S BEEN THERE

Dear Reader,

Many of you may have heard of the "It Gets Better" video campaign that started after another teen suicide linked to bullying occurred recently. Since the campaign began, over 50,000 videos have been made and posted by adults all over the world to spread the message that life gets better as you get older.

I used to hate it when adults would tell me how things would be when I got older. My feeling was, "how the heck are they supposed to know how I feel, what my life is like or what it will be like later?" But then, when I was scared about something and feeling like I couldn't talk to my parents, I would wonder why no adults could see what a hard time I was having and give me advice that would make things better.

When I was young, people were afraid to say they were gay or lesbian. Trans was not even discussed. The only way I could find out anything about gay people was to go to the library and look for books with the word homosexuality in them. There was no Internet. No Google. But when I'd find a book that I thought might tell me something about myself, I was often too afraid to even sign the check out card in case someone saw my name.

So, how could I possibly tell anyone how agonizing it was that my brother was dating one of my best friends in high school, a girl I was totally crushing on? Michele always seemed to know interesting things and ate out in real restaurants on her own. She had long silky hair that was naturally straight (back then, it was cool to iron your hair or try to sleep with it rolled up around empty orange juice cans. Pretty weird, huh?) I wanted to be the one to do interesting things with her, or go out to lunch with her, or to run my fingers through her hair. I wanted to be the one she kissed, if I could ever allow myself to have those feelings. Or at least, I wanted to see how it felt. Instead, I had to watch my brother get to do those things while I dated his friend Michael, because he was around and I thought I should be dating someone. He was nice enough I guess, but he wasn't Michele.

Who was I supposed to talk to about that? Who was I supposed to confide in and say that sometimes I felt so bad and so confused I could barely make it to school?

It sure has gotten better since then. I grew up to have a pretty good life. I have good friends and family. I have traveled all over the world. I have an artist's life writing and directing plays. I have love and fulfillment and fun. I have lived different lives and have had different kinds of romantic relationships, with women and with men. And what happened with Michele is in the past, along with most of the things that upset or hurt me so much when I was growing up.

Although sometimes I didn't think I would make it, I grew up. It got better. And I became an adult, the kind I used to hate for telling me how things would be and the kind I wished would notice me and tell me that things wouldn't always feel so bad. So here is what I think, as an adult. Take it or leave it.

I think it can be really hard to be young because you don't get to call the shots. Often you have to play by someone else's rules. I also think that sometimes adults have good ideas because they have been around long enough to see a lot. Not always, as we know. But sometimes, sometimes there is something to be said for experience.

We live in a world that is full of labels. Sometimes those labels can be helpful because they help us find ourselves. And sometimes they are really limiting. We may start out in one place and wind up in another and still another. That is ok. Your only obligation is to find what feels good and true for you and to do your best to be honest and kind to others as you are figuring things out.

I encourage you to try to figure things out. How can you know who you are if you don't try? And figuring it out with people is probably better than just looking up books in the library and then being afraid to sign them out. Or relying on Google.

Maybe you are gay or lesbian, and maybe you're uncertain. Maybe you're bi. Maybe you are trans. Whoever you are is fine. There are some wonderful people out there that identify in all kinds of ways, both young and old. Some you already know because they are public figures and are living interesting and often happy lives. Some you'd pass on the sidewalk and not even notice. And that is ok, too. I want to assure you that you don't have to be any one way to be gay, lesbian, bi, trans, or anything. You don't have to have short hair or long hair or dress in a certain way. You can just be how you feel most like yourself. Really.

But you do have to tell someone. Because if you don't, you may feel like you're the only one, like you're alone, like you're going out of your mind. Or worse, maybe even like something is wrong with you. And I can assure you, that there is nothing wrong with you.

Please choose whoever you tell carefully because you are sharing something important about yourself and you want them to be kind and supportive. Find an adult you can talk to or other LGBTQ youth that you trust and with whom you can hang. Maybe do activities together that make you feel good. Maybe even read this book together.

I am so happy that there is a book like this for you. I wish there had been a book like this when I was growing up. But there wasn't. So instead, years later, I get to contribute to it and share some of the pieces that the youth in our ensemble have done. Wow. That really does feel better.

I hope you enjoy the pieces in this book and that you make them your own when you perform them. I hope you also feel inspired to write some of your own. Like Cindy Lauper says, "You're beautiful. Like a rainbow."

And you are. So go out. Live your lives and don't be afraid. Because you're not alone. And it does get better.

Love,
Joan Lipkin

Q+A with Brian Guehring
from The Rose Theater in Omaha, NE

Brian Guehring is the Education Director/Playwright in Residence at the Omaha Theater Company for Young People at The Rose Theater. He is also the Director of Pride Players, a teen theater production of the Omaha Theater Company. Here's what he has to say about his work involving LGBTQ youth and theatre.

add**verb**: How has working to support LGBTQ youth changed or informed YOUR LIFE?

Brian Guehring: Working with Pride Players has really helped me stay positive and hopeful for the future. The young people in the cast (LGBTQ and the allies) are so energetic and feel so strongly about equal rights that I am confident that it will happen when this generation is in charge.

AV: Give a lesson learned from a difficult talk back/post show.

BG: We've learned that it is important to bring in positive religious guests to speak with our cast. Most of the experience of our teens with religion is very negative, but if the show is very anti-religion, it can offend some open-minded religious audience members who want to support the work.

AV: What's the best audience feedback you or one of your actors/shows every got?

BG: We just had an alumnus from the first Pride Players 12 years ago attend our show. He is now 27 and has joined the military and fought in Afghanistan and Iraq and is now returning to go to college. He told our cast to "realize that what you are doing is so important and changing minds. No matter where your life's journey takes you, you will always remember this experience."

AV: If you want to say something else, please do!

BG: We are looking to put a web page together with links to lots of performance content, as well as a call for more performance pieces for volume two...but that is getting ahead of the situation, I suppose.

Check out www.rosetheater.org for more information.

LGBTQ & ALLIED ORGANIZATIONS

The organizations included below are only a handful of the ones that exist. Many of them have regional chapters, and there are many, MANY regional and local organizations all over the country, and all over the world. We hope that this list is encouraging, and shows just how much action and support is out there. Want to get involved with or know more about an organization? Visit their website, or better—call them up!

NATIONAL

EQUALITY ACROSS AMERICA: The EAA National Organizing Team represents a diverse group of activists from many groups, cities and experiences. Their regional and citywide conferences across the country draw more than 1,300 LGBTQ activists and allies and allowed them to win more people to build a national grassroots network through EAA and to meet many of these new leaders.

> *Services: Annual Conferences, Grassroots organizing*

(i) equalityacrossamerica.org

GLSEN: GLSEN, the Gay, Lesbian and Straight Education Network, is the leading national education organization focused on ensuring safe schools for all students. Established in 1990, GLSEN envisions a world in which every child learns to respect and accept all people, regardless of sexual orientation or gender identity/expression. GLSEN seeks to develop school climates where difference is valued for the positive contribution it makes to creating a more vibrant and diverse community.

> *Services: Materials and support for school campaigns, Support and resources for GSA's (Gay Straight Alliances), Train the trainers*

(i) GLSEN National Headquarters
90 Broad Street, 2nd Floor
New York, NY 10004
212 727 0135
212 727 0254 *(fax)*
glsen@glsen.org
www.glsen.org

GLBT NATIONAL HELP CENTER: Providing free and confidential telephone and internet peer counseling, information and local resources for LGBTQ callers throughout the United States.

Services: Hotlines, Peer support, Online peer support chat

(i) GLBT National Help Center
2261 Market Street, PMB #296
San Francisco, CA 94114
415 355 0003
415 552 5498 *(fax)*
GLBT National Hotline: 888 843 4564
GLBT National Youth Talkline: 800 246 PRIDE (7743)
info@GLBTNationalHelpCenter.org
www.glnh.org

THE TREVOR PROJECT: The Trevor Project is the leading national organization focused on crisis and suicide prevention efforts among LGBTQ youth.

Services: 24 hour suicide hotline for LGBTQ youth, Online question forum, Chat/IM support, Social networking for LGBTQ youth, Internships, Public policy advocacy, Workshops

(i) The Trevor Lifeline 1-866-4-U-TREVOR
8704 Santa Monica Blvd., Ste. 200
West Hollywood, CA 90069
310 271 8845
310 271 8846 *(fax)*
www.thetrevorproject.org

NATIONAL GAY AND LESBIAN TASK FORCE: Building the grassroots power of the LGBTQ community. They train activists, equip state and local organizations with the skills needed to organize broad-based campaigns to defeat anti-LGBTQ referenda and advance pro-LGBTQ legislation, and build the organizational capacity of our movement. Their Policy Institute provides research and policy analysis to support the struggle for complete equality and to counter right-wing lies.

Services: Advocate training, Public policy, Research and policy analysis, Conferences

(i) National Gay and Lesbian Task Force
1325 Massachusetts Ave. NW, Suite 600
Washington, DC 20005
202 393 5177
202 393 2241 *(fax)*
www.thetaskforce.org

HUMAN RIGHTS CAMPAIGN: National LGBTQ organization that seeks equal rights on a federal level.

Services: Youth and Campus Outreach Project, Generation Equality Project, Resources and guides on a variety of topics from employment to coming out to transgender 101

(i) Human Rights Campaign
1640 Rhode Island Ave NW
Washington, DC 20036
202 628 4160
TTY: 202 216 1572
Toll-Free: 800 777 4723
202 347 5323 *(fax)*
www.hrc.org

AMERICAN CIVIL LIBERTIES UNION: The mission of the ACLU is to preserve all of these protections and guarantees: Your First Amendment, your right to equal protection under the law, your right to due process - fair treatment by the government whenever the loss of your liberty or property is at stake, and your right to privacy.

Services: Online news and blogs, Legislative updates, Activism resources and ideas

(i) www.aclu.org

COLAGE is a national movement of children, youth, and adults with one or more LGBTQ parent/s. They build community and work toward social justice through youth empowerment, leadership development, education, and advocacy.

> *Services: Resources and publications, E-groups, Email alerts, Events, Connect with local chapters*

(i) COLAGE
1550 Bryant Street, Suite 830
San Francisco, CA 94103
415 867 5437
colage@colage.org
www.colage.org

THE GAY & LESBIAN ALLIANCE AGAINST DEFAMATION (GLAAD) amplifies the voice of the LGBTQ community by empowering real people to share their stories, holding the media accountable for the words and images they present, and helping grassroots organizations communicate effectively. By ensuring that the stories of LGBTQ people are heard through the media, GLAAD promotes understanding, increases acceptance, and advances equality.

> *Services: Resources and publications, Email action alerts, Blogs and commentary about current events and media, Talking About series materials, Resources and publications, Email action alerts, Blogs and commentary about current events and media, Talking About series materials*

(i) GLAAD
5455 Wilshire Blvd, #1500, Los Angeles, CA 90036
323 933 2240
323 933-2241 *(fax)*

104 West 29th Street, 4th Fl, New York, NY 10001
212 629 3322
212 629-3225 *(fax)*
info@glaad.org
www.glaad.org

GAY AND LESBIAN MEDICAL ASSOCIATION: GLMA's mission is to ensure equality in health care for LGBTQ individuals and health care providers.

Services: Resources and publications, Online medical provider directory, Lesbian Health Fund, Training for medical providers

Gay and Lesbian Medical Association
1326 18th Street NW, Suite 22
Washington, DC 20036
202 600 8037
202 478 1500 *(fax)*
info@glma.org
www.glma.org

LAMBDA LEGAL: A national organization committed to achieving full recognition of the civil rights of LGBTQ people and those with HIV through impact litigation, education and public policy work.

Services: Legal resources, Events, Online resources and publications

Lambda Legal
120 Wall Street, Suite 1500
New York, NY 10005
212 809 8585
212 809 0055 *(fax)*
www.lambdalegal.org

THE NATIONAL YOUTH ADVOCACY COALITION (NYAC):
A social justice organization that advocates for and with young LGBTQ people in an effort to end discrimination against these youth and to ensure their physical and emotional well-being.

Services: Email updates, Capacity Building, Advocacy, Resources for engaging and empowering LGBTQ youth

(i) NYAC
1638 R Street, NW, Suite 300
Washington, DC 20009
Toll Free: 800 541 6922
202 319 7596
877 492 8916 *(fax)*
nyac@nyacyouth.org
nyacyouth.org

**PARENTS, FAMILIES AND FRIENDS OF LESBIANS AND GAYS
(PFLAG)** promotes the health and well-being of LGBTQ persons, their
families and friends through: support, to cope with an adverse society;
education, to enlighten an ill-informed public; and advocacy, to end
discrimination and to secure equal civil rights. Parents, Families and
Friends of Lesbians and Gays provides opportunity for dialogue about
sexual orientation and gender identity, and acts to create a society that is
healthy and respectful of human diversity.

> *Services: Resources and links, Local chapters, Email action
> alerts, Safe Schools for All program, Online newsroom,
> Multilingual resources*

(i) PFLAG National Office
1828 L Street, NW, Suite 660
Washington, DC 20036
202 467 8180
202 349 0788 *(fax)*
info@pflag.org
www.pflag.org

THE SAFE SCHOOLS COALITION is an international public-private
partnership in support of LGBTQ youth, that is working to help schools -
at home and all over the world - become safe places where every family
can belong, where every educator can teach, and where every child can
learn, regardless of gender identity or sexual orientation.

Services: Speakers' bureau, Online resources and publications, Classroom resources, Listserve, Reports and posters, Crisis line (WA only)

(i) Safe Schools Coalition
c/o Rosehedge
115 - 16th Avenue
Seattle, WA 98122
24-hour Crisis Phone for SSC Intervention Team:
(Washington State only) 877 SAFE SAFE (877 723 3723)
www.safeschoolscoalition.org

TRUE COLORS is a non-profit organization that works with other social service agencies, schools, organizations, and within communities to ensure that the needs of sexual and gender minority youth are both recognized and competently met.

Services: Scholarships, Conferences and events, Mentoring program, Training and seminars, Email list

(i) True Colors, Inc.
576 Farmington Avenue
Hartford, CT 06105
860 232 0050
860 232 0049 *(fax)*
director@ourtruecolors.org
True Colors Conference: conference@ourtruecolors.org
Workshops, Trainings & Seminars: director@ourtruecolors.org
The Safe Harbor Project: safeharbor@ourtruecolors.org
ourtruecolors.org

TEACHING TOLERANCE: Founded in 1991 by the Southern Poverty Law Center, Teaching Tolerance is dedicated to reducing prejudice, improving intergroup relations and supporting equitable school experiences for our nation's children.

Services: Magazine, Professional Development, Classroom Activities, Teaching Kits

(i) Teaching Tolerance
A Project of the Southern Poverty Law Center
400 Washington Ave.
Montgomery, AL 36104
334 956 8200
www.tolerance.org

OUTHEALTH! works to improve access to and the quality of care for LGBTQ adults.

Services: Tools and materials, Technical assistance

(i) OutHealth!
Health Imperatives
942 W Chestnut Street
Brockton, MA 02301
800 530 2770
508 583 2611 *(fax)*
mhoward-karp@hcsm.org
www.hcsm.org/outhealth

THE LAMBDA 10 PROJECT - National Clearinghouse for LGBTQ Fraternity & Sorority Issues works to heighten the visibility of LGBTQ members of the college fraternity by serving as a clearinghouse for educational resources and educational materials related to sexual orientation and gender identity/expression as it pertains to the fraternity/sorority experience.

Services: Out and Greek conference, Resources and publications, Social networking

Lambda 10 Project
National Clearinghouse for GLBT Fraternity & Sorority Issues
PO Box 240473
Charlotte, NC 28224
704 277 6710
704 553 1639 *(fax)*
info@lambda10.org
www.lambda10.org

CAMPUS PRIDE represents the only national nonprofit 501(c)(3) organization for student leaders and campus groups working to create a safer college environment for LGBTQ students. The organization is a volunteer-driven network "for" and "by" student leaders. The primary objective of Campus Pride is to develop necessary resources, programs and services to support LGBTQ and ally students on college campuses across the United States.

> *Services: Events, Resources and publications, Reports, Camp Pride, Blog and news, College fairs*

Campus Pride
PO Box 240473
Charlotte, NC 28224
704 277 6710
704 553 1639 *(fax)*
info@campuspride.org
www.campuspride.org

CENTERLINK exists to support the development of strong, sustainable LGBTQ community centers and to build a unified center movement.

> *Services: Newsletter, Action alerts, Capacity building, technical assistance, leadership development, Executive directors' conference*

CenterLink
PO Box 24490
Fort Lauderdale, FL 33307
954 765 6024
954 765 6593 *(fax)*
CenterLink@lgbtcenters.org
www.lgbtcenters.org

FAMILY PRIDE works at all levels of government to advance full social and legal equality on behalf of the approximately one million LGBTQ families raising two million children. Parenting protections, adoption, repeal of the so-called Defense of Marriage Act, health insurance reform, immigration reform, safe schools, and workplace equality are many of the issues Family Equality Council is currently working on at the state and federal level.

> *Services: Resources, Public policy, Events, Publications and reports, Blog*

Family Equality Council
PO Box 206
Boston, MA 02133
617 502 8700
617 502 8701 *(fax)*
info@familyequality.org
www.familypride.org

YOUTHRESOURCE is a Web site created by and for GLBTQ young people. YouthResource takes a holistic approach to sexual health and exploring issues of concern to GLBTQ youth, by providing information and offer support on sexual and reproductive health issues through education and advocacy. Through monthly features, message boards, and online peer education, GLBTQ youth receive information on activism, culture, sexual health, and other issues that are important to them.

Services: Peer education, Information and referrals, Events, Blog

(i) Advocates for Youth
2000 M Street NW, Suite 750
Washington, DC 20036
202 419 3420
www.amplifyyourvoice.org/youthresource

POINT FOUNDATION provides financial support, mentoring, leadership training and hope to meritorious students who are marginalized due to sexual orientation, gender identity or gender expression.

Services: Scholarships, Mailing List, Events, Mentoring

(i) Point Foundation
323 933 1234
866 33 POINT (866 337 6468)
866 39 POINT (866-397-6468) *(fax)*
info@pointfoundation.org
www.pointfoundation.org

GSA NETWORK supports GSAs--student organizations, found primarily in North American high schools and universities that are intended to provide a safe and supportive environment for LGBTQ youth and their allies.

Services: News, Events, Resources, Email list, Regional chapters

(i) GSA Network
1550 Bryant Street, Suite 800
San Francisco, CA 94103
415 552 4229
info@gsanetwork.org
gsanetwork.org

THE GAY, LESBIAN, BISEXUAL, TRANSGENDER HISTORICAL SOCIETY is a museum and archives of material relating to the history of LGBTQ people in the United States, with a focus on the LGBTQ communities of San Francisco and Northern California.

Services: E-newsletter, Museum, Video archives, Reading room, Archives, E-newsletter, Museum, Video archives

(i) GLBT Historical Society
657 Mission Street #300
San Francisco, CA 94105
415 777 5455
415 777 5576 *(fax)*
info@glbthistory.org
www.glbthistory.org

TRANSLATE GENDER: Translate Gender is a collective-based consensus-run nonprofit organization that works to generate community accountability for individuals to self-determine their own genders and gender expressions. Translate provides workshops, consultation, mediation, and facilitation focused on gender oppression and concerns specific to trans and/or gender non-conforming individuals. *(Check out their Identity Spectrums pinwheel on pg.186)*

(i) 121 Fifth Avenue, PMB 131
Brooklyn, NY 11217
www.translategender.org

MASSACHUSETTS AREA & NATIONAL

✡ **KESHET'S** mission is to ensure that LGBTQ Jews are fully included in all parts of the Jewish community. In the Greater Boston area, Keshet offers social and cultural events for GLBTQ Jews ranging from Jewish text study to an annual GLBTQ Jewish speed-dating gala, Keshet Quick Dates. Nationally, Keshet offers support, training, and resources to create a Jewish community that welcomes and affirms GLBTQ Jews.

Services: Hineini education project, Resources and publications, Film screenings and workshops, KeshetClal inclusion project

(i) KESHET
284 Amory Street
Jamaica Plain, MA 02130
617 524 9227
617 524 9229 *(fax)*
info@keshetonline.org
www.keshetonline.org

NORTHWEST AREA & NATIONAL

PRIDE FOUNDATION inspires a culture of generosity that connects and strengthens Northwest organizations, leaders, and students who are creating LGBTQ equality.

Services: Grants, Scholarships, Regional organizing, Blog

(i) Pride Foundation
1122 E Pike Street PMB 1001 *(mailing address)*
Seattle, WA 98122
Toll Free: 800 735 7287
206 323 3318
www.pridefoundation.org

INTERNATIONAL

INTERPRIDE is the international association for organizations that produce Pride Events around the world. Our member organizations are dedicated to producing Pride events for the global LGBTQ community.

Services: Annual conference, Newsletter, Resources for Pride celebration organizers

info@interpride.org
www.interpride.org

AMNESTY INTERNATIONAL: OUTfront! Campaign: Lesbian, Gay, Bisexual and Transgender Human Rights

Services: Demand Dignity campaign, International LGBTQ social justice resources and information

www.amnesty.org/en

GAY AND LESBIAN ARABIC SOCIETY (GLAS): International organization established in 1988 in the USA with worldwide chapters. They serve as a networking organization for Gays and Lesbians of Arab descent or those living in Arab countries. They aim to promote positive images of Gays and Lesbians in Arab communities worldwide, in addition to combating negative portrayals of Arabs within the Gay and Lesbian community. We also provide a support network for our members while fighting for our human rights wherever they are oppressed. We are part of the global Gay and Lesbian movement seeking an end to injustice and discrimination based on sexual orientation.

Services: Mailing list, Articles, Entertainment, Local chapters

www.glas.org

LGBTQ & ALLIED PLACES, SPACES & FACES

Pride Youth Theater Alliance (PYTA)

PYTA connects and supports queer youth theater organizations, programs, and professionals committed to empowering lesbian, gay, bisexual, transgender, queer and allied (LGBTQA) youth in North America: www.prideyouththeateralliance.org

PYTA Member Organizations

About Face Theater

About Face is an identity affirming theatre activism program based at Chicago, Illinois.
> Visit: www.aboutfacetheatre.com

add**verb** Productions/University of New England

Out & Allied is a youth writing project which uses the power of performance to communicate and educate.
> Visit: www.addverbproductions.org/programs/outallied

Buddies in Bad Times Theatre: Queer Youth Arts Program

Buddies in Bad Times Theatre creates theatre by developing and presenting voices that question sexual and cultural norms. Built on the political and social principles of queer liberation, Buddies supports artists and works that reflect and advance these values.
> Visit: buddiesinbadtimes.com/youth

Creative Action: Outside the Lines Youth Theatre Ensemble

Outside the Lines is part of a Creative Action partnership with Out Youth and the University of Texas Department of Theatre and Dance. Out Youth's mission is to promote the physical, mental, emotional, spiritual and social well being of sexual and gender minority youth so that they can openly and safely explore and affirm their identities.
> Visit: creativeaction.org/programs/youth-ensembles

Dreams of Hope

Formed in 2003 to develop LGBTQ youth leaders who educate audiences about issues they face, each performance includes a youth led discussion.
> Visit: www.dreamsofhope.org/programs

Fringe Benefits

Fringe Benefits is a groundbreaking educational theatre company whose workshops and productions have earned the commendations of youth, educators, parents and community leaders.
> Visit: www.cootieshots.org/

Gay and Lesbian Service Organization (GSO): Company Q

Company Q is a unique performance/ social justice theatre troupe for young people focusing on queer issues. It is based at the Gay and Lesbian Service Organization in Lexington, Kentucky.
> Visit: www.facebook.com/companyqlexington

Lifeworks, LA Gay & Lesbian Center: Outset Theater

LifeWorks and Outfest, two independent non-profit organizations working together nurtures and inspires aspiring young filmmakers. OutSet provides participants with access to and guidance by working professional mentors from the film and television industries.
> Visit: lifeworksla.org/outset/index.html

The Neutral Zone: Riot Youth

Riot Youth, a program for LGBTQ teens operates out of The Neutral Zone in Ann Arbor, Michigan. Through leadership skill building, community organizing, networking, and socializing, Riot Youth connects youth to build an inclusive community. Teens also engage in social justice through theater, dialogue, lobbying and other advocacy efforts.
> Visit: www.neutral-zone.org

The New Conservatory Theatre Center: YouthAware Out & United (Y.O.U.)

Y.O.U. provides LGBTQI teens and their allies an empowered voice though theater, as well as provide a safe and welcoming venue for sharing their stories, triumphs, and concerns about being a lesbian, gay, bi-sexual, transgender, questioning, or straight allied teen in the Bay Area.
> Visit: www.nctcsf.org/you.htm

New Orleans Queer Youth Theater Project

The New Orleans Queer Youth Theater is a space where youth can explore varied and fluid performances of queerness, harness their voice and power through theater making techniques, and hang out with other queer and allied youth.
Visit: www.facebook.com/pages/
New-Orleans-Queer-Youth-Theater/145327728986491

Oakland Center for the Arts: YOUnify Theatre Company
Developed through a Mukti Fund grant, YOUnify provides the place
for all Queer Youth of the Mahoning Valley to tell their stories through
theatre, music and art.
> Visit: oaklandcenter.com

Omaha Theater Company at the Rose: Pride Players
Pride Players uses improvisation to create songs, poetry, monologues,
and skits that explore what it means to be a gay, lesbian, bisexual,
transgendered, or straight-allied teen in Omaha.
> Visit: www.rosetheater.org/classes-programs/
        2013-14-teen-season/pride-players-project-15

Proud Theater
Proud Theater is open to 13-19 year-old LGBTQ youth, children of
LGBTQ parents, or allies of the LGBTQ community. This innovate
theatre program allows the youth to tell their own stories and is designed
to foster self-expression and self-empowerment for youth around the state
of Wisconsin.
> Visit: www.proudtheater.org

Rainbow Pride Youth Alliance: FIERCE (RPYA)
PRYA provides a safe, healthy, and enriching environment for LGBTQI
youth in Ontario, Riverside, and San Bernardino in Southern California.
RPYA is a safe haven where youth are supported and challenged to engage
fully in their own personal, social, and artistic development. FIERCE is a
peer-led wellness strategy designed to introduce youth and their families
to the power of art, enhancing communication across generations and
building a stronger community and neighborhood. Theater is used as a tool
for enhancing self-esteem, developing language and communication skills,
strengthening cultural identity, increasing academic and vocational skill
sets, and promoting literacy.
> Visit: www.rpya-ie.org

The Coterie Theatre: Project Pride
LGBTQ and straight allied teens creates theatre that gives voice to
their experiences, culminating in a production that challenges the
assumptions and celebrates the diversity of the participants and audience. Project Pride is guided by: Love, Generosity, Beauty, Truth.
> Visit: thecoterie.org

The Queer Youth Theater at The Door (QYT)
Based in New York City, The Queer Youth Theater creates original pieces using the ideas and concerns of young people in the group. QYT meets at The Door, a comprehensive youth services organization in Manhattan. The group is primarily intended for LGBTQIA youth, but includes straight allies.
> Visit: www.facebook.com/pages/
      The-Queer-Youth-Theater/244446522294077

The GLBT Community Center of Colorado:
Rainbow Alley Theater Program
This program teaches youth to perform scripted and self-scripted theatrical works for the greater community. The philosophy of the program is to support youth in the development of amplifying their voice and refining their craft, while addressing the serious issues that LGBTQ youth face, including bullying, rejection by families, home- lessness, discrimination, violence, depression, and suicide.
> Visit: www.glbtcolorado.org/rainbow-alley/
      rainbow-alley-programs-and-services

The Theater Offensive: True Colors: Out Youth Theater
Provides year-round theater programming for lesbian, gay, bisexual, transgender, queer and questioning youth and their straight allies (LGBTQQA), ages 14 to 22. Dedicated to presenting an honest portrayal of the lives of LGBTQQA youth through group playwriting, production, performance and theater training intensives.
> Visit: www.thetheateroffensive.org/?page_id=2970

Theater Askew Youth Performance Experience (TAYPE)
An educational theatre program that empowers lesbian, gay, bisexual, transgender, and questioning (LGBTQ) youth and their allies in the New York area by nurturing and developing their unique theatrical voices.
> Visit: www.theatreaskew.com/taype.htm

Theatre UCF and Zebra Coalition: interACTionZ
An all-inclusive youth theatre partnership between Orlando Repertory
Theatre, Theatre UCF, and the Zebra Coalition in Orlando, Florida. This
hands-on and thought-provoking program is designed for LGBTQ+ youth
and youth who identify as straight advocates for the LGBTQ+ community.
interACTionZ focuses on using theatre for social change techniques in
order to build community, creatively explore conflict-resolution, and
develop youth leadership skills.
> Visit: www.facebook.com/interACtionZ

Waterville Inclusive Community Project: Out & Allied Youth Theatre
Established through Mukti's Queer Youth Theater Incubator Fund, a core
of LGBTQ youth and their allies will perform, direct and write original
performance pieces to create change in their schools and communities.
Visit: wicpme.wordpress.com/2013/07/06/
       pride-youth-theater-alliance-grant/

PERFORMANCE PIECES BY THEME

Many of these pieces are readily adaptable to reflect different sexual orientations, biological sex, gender identity or gender expression. Please feel free to make changes that also honor the intentions of the writers.

Acceptance
Absolving Yesterday by Jake Johansen ....Page 82
If I Speak by Rob Greatness ....Page 57
Understand by Anonymous Youth Artists Team ....Page 4
Jeopardy by Elyse Spike Johnson ....Page 85
Tea With Dad by Cathy Plourde ....Page 128
Rationalizing by Shawna Searles ....Page 26
Tough Guys Wear Pink by Stephen M. Feest ....Page 136
Proud by Lauren Kidd ....Page 2
Our Uttermost Important Gift by Kayla Cowan ....Page 24

Being an Ally
Rationalizing by Shawna Searles ....Page 26
What Makes a Man? By Micah Malenfant ....Page 102

Being Silenced
Wishes by Bells ....Page 21
If I Speak by Rob Greatness ....Page 57

Bullying
Throwing by Joan Lipkin and the Apple Pie Ensemble, created under the auspices of That Uppity Theatre Company ....Page 11
The Serpent by Megan E. Jackson ....Page 103
Once Again by Elyse Spike Johnson ....Page 125
Run Away by Brianna Suslovic ....Page 100
To The Boy Who Yelled Faggot Outside Wildcatessen a Few Weeks Ago by Marie Coyle ....Page 54

Courage
The Girl I Kiss in Bus Seats by Marianna Bueti ....Page 93
A Phone Call by Rai Silverstein ....Page 8

Crushing Out
I'm Not Gay, But Thanks! By Meredith Lamothe ....Page 65

Development
The Crayola Crusade by John Coons ....Page 17
We Fly Like Butterflies in Harmonic Symphony by Kayla Cowan ....Page 62
Personals by Joan Lipkin and the Apple Pie Ensemble, created under the auspices of That Uppity Theatre Company ....Page 70

Family
For The Rest of My Life by Andrew Cole ....Page 42
After Breakfast by Meghan Brodie ....Page 47

Friendship
Linda by Joan Lipkin ....Page 121

Gender Queer
Grey by Mea Tavares ....Page 58
Liquid Gender Form by Stephen M. Feest ....Page 96

Homophobia
Understand by Anonymous Youth Artists Team ....Page 4
Dining Out by Vianca Yohn ....Page 34
Run Away by Brianna Suslovic ....Page 100

Humor
Sock it to Me, Baby by Cathy Plourde ....Page 88

Love
A Phone Call by Rai Silverstein ....Page 8
Our Uttermost Important Gift by Kayla Cowan ....Page 24
Erin by Elizabeth Peek/Wykes ....Page 46
Natural Stance by Victoria Baker ....Page 126

Pride
Proud by Lauren Kidd ....Page 2

Questioning

After Breakfast by Meghan Brodie ....Page 47

The Serpent by Megan E. Jackson ....Page 103

The Straightest Gay Guy in the World by Micah Malenfant ....Page 30

Safe Space

To The Boy Who Yelled Faggot Outside Wildcatessen a Few Weeks Ago
by Marie Coyle ....Page 54

Serious

Pain by Alex Eisenhart ....Page 72

Wishes by Bells ....Page 21

If I Speak by Rob Greatness ....Page 57

Stereotypes

The Straightest Gay Guy in the World by Micah Malenfant ....Page 30

Liquid Gender Form by Stephen M. Feest ....Page 96

Tough Guys Wear Pink by Stephen M. Feest ....Page 136

Once Again by Elyse Spike Johnson ....Page 125

Trans

Tranny Next Door by Carrie-Lynne Davis, adapted by Deacon Lasagna
and Ellis Matthews ....Page 74

ABOUT add**verb**

Cathy Plourde founded add**verb** in 2000 and began presenting programs, plays and workshops that used theatre and arts in social change — health and wellness, advocacy, and justice.

Formally incorporating in 2003, add**verb's** signature programs *The Thin Line* and *You the Man* traveled the US. These one-actor, multi-character shows sat in the middle of an education and community-action program, which addressed coping with eating disorders, or engaging bystanders in preventing dating and sexual violence. add**verb** collaborated or initiated several programs; contracted and/or trained teaching artists; and supported individuals and organizations with fiscal sponsorship.

The *Out & Allied* project began in 2008 and has been fueled by intern and youth efforts. In 2011, add**verb** was acquired by the University of New England (Maine, USA) sharing a vision of innovative approaches to health and wellness education. During tenure at UNE the youth-driven Out & Allied Project netted two volumes of materials, dozens of performances and workshops, and hundreds in the audiences in Maine. Importantly, the volumes reflect a synchronicity of work being done with queer and allied youth around the US and in Canada, much of which was funded by the Mukti Fund as well as other generous forward thinking LGBTQ, Youth, Arts, and Community-Building funders. These volumes document a great deal of hope, strength and courage, evidence of youth taking their stories, lives, challenges and strategies to the stage.

At this writing add**verb**'s programs and projects are no longer formally organized within an institution, but are available through licensing, publishing, or open-source.

www.addverbproductions.org
www.outandallied.org

www.ingramcontent.com/pod-product-compliance
Lightning Source LLC
LaVergne TN
LVHW051625080426
835511LV00016B/2176